The
Eleventh
Hour

BY THE SAME AUTHOR

The Book of Certainty
A Sufi Saint of the Twentieth Century: Shaykh Aḥmad al-ʿAlawī
Symbol and Archetype: A Study of the Meaning of Existence
Ancient Beliefs and Modern Superstitions
What is Sufism?
The Qur'anic Art of Calligraphy and Illumination
Muhammad: His Life based on the Earliest Sources
The Secret of Shakespeare
Collected Poems
Splendours of Qur'an Calligraphy and Illumination
Sufi Poems: A Mediaeval Anthology
Mecca: From before Genesis until Now
A Return to the Spirit: Questions and Answers
The Holy Qur'an: Translations of Selected Verses

The Eleventh Hour

The Spiritual Crisis of the Modern World in the Light of Tradition and Prophecy

Martin Lings

This edition first published in 2002 by
Archetype
Chetwynd House
Bartlow
Cambridge CB21 4PP, UK

ISBN 978 1 901383 01 0

British Library Cataloguing in Publication Data
A catalogue record for this book is available from
the British Library

Typeset by Colin Etheridge
Printed and bound in Great Britain by
TJ International Ltd, Padstow, Cornwall

CONTENTS

Preface

ACCORDING to an ancient and still recognized legal principle an accused man cannot plead, in his defence, ignorance of the law; and since in the older civilizations the temporal and the spiritual were organically connected, this principle may well have originated as a prolongation of the dogma that on the Day of Judgement it will not be possible to plead ignorance of the basic truths of religion.

The dogma in question is to be found expressed, implicitly or explicitly, in various ways. Islam, for example, is particularly explicit: in the Qur'ān, God is said to have taken to Himself, out of the loins of Adam, the seeds of all future generations of men and to have put to them the question: 'Am I not your Lord?', to which they answered in the affirmative. The Qur'ān adds that they were made to testify, 'lest ye should say on the Day of Resurrection: "Verily, of this we were unaware"'.

In other words, every human soul is imbued with what might be called the sense of the Absolute or of the Transcendent, the sense of a Supreme Power that is both Origin and End of the created universe which It infinitely transcends. This sense belongs to the faculty of the Intellect, which is man's means of perceiving what lies above and beyond the plane of his world; and though the full power of the intellect was lost at the Fall, what remains of its light is nonetheless sufficiently strong to be undeniable, as the above Qur'ānic verse makes clear. This residue of heart knowledge—for the Intellect is enthroned in the Heart[1]—is man's highest faculty, and may still be termed intellect if only in a relative sense. Its

[1] This word is written here with a capital to indicate that it means, not the bodily heart, but the centre of the soul, that is, the point through which passes the vertical axis in virtue of which man is Mediator between Heaven and earth.

survival does not however prevent the refusal to see it—a refusal which can become second nature. 'Hardness of heart' was originally the name of the chronic blindness in question.

In the 'Dark Ages' students were taught that the faculties are ranged in hierarchy, of which the summit is Intellect, inasmuch as it is concerned with transcendent realities, whereas reason, which ranks as a subordinate second to it, is limited to this world. Since 'the Enlightenment' however the Intellect in its original sense has been withdrawn from the attention of students; but the word itself, brought down from the supernatural level, has been retained in virtue of its high-sounding effect. In particular, its much used adjective has now taken on the sense of 'mentally active'; and since much of the activity is concerned with questioning the existence of the transcendent,[2] many of the so called 'intellectuals' are at the opposite pole from true intellectuality. The confusion is so widespread that it would seem a great paradox—and yet it would be true—to say that religious faith, of all that is now 'officially' recognized as a human possibility, comes nearest to intellectual awareness, though it must be admitted that the two do not coincide unless we understand faith in its higher sense of certitude.

Robbed of its name, the intellect still subsists, which means that there is still something in man which is incorruptible and inviolable, a supramental organ of knowledge which, unlike the mind, is proof against error. It follows from this that sincerity,

[2] One aspect of the transcendent which is most frequently called in question is the miraculous. To deny miracles is thought to be intelligent and even intellectual. In reality such a denial results from an exceedingly unintelligent rationalism. A glimmering of intellectuality would make it clear that miracles are inevitable if there is to be any operative bond or link—and that is what the word religion means—between God and man. 'If we term "natural" that which simply obeys the logic of things, the supernatural is also natural, but it is so in a scale far vaster than that of physical causality, that of this lower world. The supernatural is the "divinely natural" which, irrupting into an eminently contingent and limited plane of the natural, contradicts the laws of this plane . . . in virtue of a far less contingent and limited causality. If "God exists"—really and fully and not as some unconscious and passive power as the naturalists and deists would have it—then miracles cannot not be.' (Frithjof Schuon, *From the Divine to the Human*, p.112)

which today is so often proffered as an excuse for error, or as a mitigating circumstance for it, is in fact incompatible with it, for sincerity worthy of the name presupposes total adherence, and there can be no such totality if one part is dormant. By way of example, to speak of a 'sincere atheist' is to utter a contradiction in terms, for the person in question is quite literally 'not all there'. If he were, or even if there were a particle of intellect vibrant within him, he could never assent to such an absolute denial of that which the heart knows to be true, theism being the very substance of man's heart. Admittedly, the atheist is an extreme case; but in a world where the prevailing ideas are exclusively 'horizontal', without any dimension of height or of depth, the odds against the intellect are considerable, that is, against its becoming effectively operative in any given individual. It is however by no means always totally dormant, and this explains the widespread doubts and perplexities of the modern world where many, perhaps even the majority, are in a state of more or less passively following a trend of thought which deep within themselves, they suspect to be wrong—'houses divided against themselves'. To describe this division as the conflict between mental persuasion and heart knowledge would be along the right lines, but in most cases the word 'knowledge' would be too strong, for there is no more than a glimmering on the side of truth.

The following chapters are an attempt to fan the flame of that glimmering and thus to restore the lost balance, first of all by seeking to persuade minds that they have nothing to lose and everything to gain from a re-establishment of the normal hierarchic relationships. The reason must become once more conscious of its need for the guidance of a higher authority—an authority which is not, however, subjectively other than it, inasmuch as both intellect and reason are different reaches of the same intelligence, the same ray of light proceeding from the Divine Truth. But the theoretic or virtual restoration of the hierarchy is no more than a beginning, albeit a necessary one. As to its actualization, that is only possible on certain conditions, which cannot be set aside; and this book's main purpose is to point the way to their fulfilment.

1

Signs of the Times

FOR THE LAST two thousand years there has been no century that did not expect shortly 'the end of the world', whatever these words are thought to mean. Already in 40 BC Virgil wrote that the end of the Iron Age was near and that a new Golden Age was soon to begin; and Hinduism has long been awaiting the rider on the white horse, Kalki, the tenth Avatara of Vishnu, who is to close the present 'Dark Age' and inaugurate a new era of perfection. Maitreya, no less eagerly awaited by the Buddhists, is clearly none other than the Kalki Avatara, and the same may be said of the Messiah.[1] It is true that in the monotheistic religions, all three of which expect the Messiah, the end of the present cycle is mainly identified with the end of time itself, that is, with Doomsday. But the concept of the Millennium none the less makes it possible to think of the end in a less absolute sense, which is in conformity with the more ancient expectation of a new cycle to follow the close of this, for the Millennium may be considered as the equivalent of the new 'reign of Saturn' which Virgil hymned.[2] As to the signs which will precede it, all traditions agree that they are exceedingly negative, though not, as we shall see, to the exclusion of signs which attain to the opposite extreme.

An event so tremendous as the birth of Christ was bound to radiate presentiments beyond the frontiers of the Semitic world. It

[1] This would seem to be confirmed by Revelation XIX, 11: 'And I saw heaven opened, and behold a white horse . . .'

[2] Ecologue IV, 6, *Redeunt Saturnia regna.*

is therefore not unreasonable to qualify as 'Messianic' the poem in which Virgil makes his prediction. What seems to have been expected by no one is the twofold aspect of the advent in question. It was not foreseen that the final triumphant coming would be heralded by a first coming which would not mark the end but only announce it. For the Jews this meant that the Messiah had not yet come in any sense, but they continued to expect him soon; and the final advent was believed by early Christians to be very near indeed, with good reason as they thought, for it seemed to them that Jesus had spoken of it as being not far off. Some six hundred years later, the Qur'ān affirmed that 'the Hour', the promised end, was 'near', and that 'the heavens and the earth are pregnant with it'; and even in the early days of the caliphate it was sometimes said to a caliph; 'Mayst thou live long enough, sire, to give thy kingdom into the hands of Jesus, the son of Mary'. Nor would any early Muslim have believed that today, after 1400 years of Islam, the end would still not yet have come, although the Qur'ān affirms that 'verily a day in the sight of thy Lord is as a thousand years of what ye count'. Despite this reservation, and despite the Biblical equivalent for Jews and Christians, 'a thousand years in Thy sight are but as yesterday', the expectations continued, century after century. They did not however remain at the same degree of intensity. In the Middle Ages, the acuteness of consciences engendered a collective sense of guilt which made it seem that the predicted signs of the second coming had already been fulfilled and that humanity had indeed reached its lowest ebb. According to Jewish, Christian and Islamic belief, the immediate threshold of the reign of the Messiah will be the tyranny of the Antichrist; and more than one prominent mediaeval figure was wrongly identified, in widespread opinion, with that greatest of malefactors. But it would no doubt be true to say, at any rate as regards the West, that the last three centuries before this were increasingly less expectant of the end. The gradual weakening of faith and the consequent lessening of attention paid to the

Scriptures were aggravated by self-satisfaction at the so-called 'Renaissance' and, in the eighteenth century, at the so-called 'Enlightenment'. It is also in the nature of things that expectation, prolonged beyond a certain point, should begin to flag.

What then of the present century? Today belief in God and the Scriptures tends to be weaker than ever; and for Westerners it has largely been replaced by agnosticism, not to speak of the atheism which, until the recent fall of communism, had been systematically indoctrinated into children from an early age in vast tracts of earthly territory. Nor is the widespread belief in evolution and progress conducive to thinking along the same lines as our ancestors thought. We might therefore presume the Western world to be correspondingly less expectant of the end today than ever it was before. But is it? The answer is clearly no. There is, however, a marked difference between the present and the past in this respect. In the past it was concluded that the end must be near, but its immanence was not felt. Today the grounds for conviction have been largely set aside or forgotten; but the end is 'in the air', existentially sensed. It is as if the souls and bodies of men were woven of finality. This is undoubtedly one of the great signs of the times; and it coincides with other signs which are less dependant upon intuition and which, in a wide variety of ways, address themselves to reason, celestial signs relating to prophecies,[3] visions and auditions, and signs which may be called human, in an individual or a political sense. These terrestrial signs—or some of them—are, respectively, the themes of two subsequent chapters; but it must first be made clear why it is important to be aware of these signs and to recognize them for what they are.

[3] Such as the famous twelfth-century prophecy of St Malachy about the Popes, according to which the end is to come in the reign of the next Pope but one. For a study we have made of this prophecy, see Appendix D. This sign may be said to appeal to the reason in that most of its predictions, that is, all those which are related to things now past, have already proved themselves to be true.

2

The Vineyard and the Marketplace

THE SENSE of the transcendent, which is an essential aspect of the human intelligence, implies, by inevitable extension, the consciousness of a need to transcend the limitations of this earthly state. The aim and end of religion in an exoteric sense is salvation which means, ultimately, Paradise and therefore transcendence. But the exoterist is one in whom the higher reaches[1] of the intelligence are dormant. He needs to be told to do this and not to do that on the basis of trust in Providence to fulfil, on condition of those pious acts and abstentions, the promise of salvation. His sense of the transcendent is limited to belief in a Supreme Power on the one hand, and on the other hand the innate desire 'to live happily ever afterwards'.[2] But unlike the esoterist he does not have already in this life the presentiment of higher states.

'The Kingdom of Heaven is within you.' This truth is the basis

[1] Or inner reaches, for there is a spiritual coincidence between height and inwardness or depth.

[2] Children are in some respects wiser than their parents, and many children are unwilling to accept a story which does not lead up to the most positive of conclusions. Nor should the significance of this childly scruple be underestimated, for the desire implicit in it is not just a naive piece of wishful thinking, as those who have stifled it in themselves like to think. Desire is summed up, in the depth of every human soul, by the longing for perfect happiness that will not end. To maintain otherwise is hypocrisy; and the fact of this universal desire is a 'proof'—not by logic in the ordinary sense but by what might be called intellectual logic that man was made for Paradise and that his true homeland is not here. The same fact is therefore, by extension, a 'proof' of the truth of religion.

of esoterism, the science and discipline of inwardness; and the aspiration of the esoterist goes beyond salvation to sanctification, which in its highest sense is deification, that is, union (the Hindu *yoga*) with the Absolute Infinite Perfection of the Divine Essence. This extinction of all relativity is the *nirvāna* of Buddhism; and in Islamic mysticism the saying 'the Sufi is not created' testifies to the same Ultimate Reality.

Christ's affirmation of the truth of the inwardness of Heaven must be taken together with his promise: 'Seek and ye shall find; knock, and it shall be opened unto you'. But despite the perpetual validity of the guarantee here given, the arduousness of the search is bound to vary from age to age; and since in ours it appears on the surface to be, in some respects, particularly formidable, a reminder that tradition has promised hidden compensations will not be out of place.

I have already considered this elsewhere[3] with special reference to 'the labourers in the vineyard'. According to the parable,[4] those who began work only at the eleventh hour received the same wage as those who had 'borne the burden and the heat of the day'. The latecomers were moreover the first to be paid. To develop now the question in more detail than before, it must be remembered that the parable is led up to by a sharp distinction between exoterism and esoterism, namely the incident of the rich young man whose attachment to his wealth disqualified him for the inner life. Esoterism is set before us in its aspect of total commitment which, it is promised, will always receive its due reward. 'But many that are first shall be last; and the last shall be first.'[5] Then follows the parable, to illustrate this reservation. It does not however explain it; the paradox is reiterated, but something of an enigma remains, though a partial key to it lies in the way in which esoterism is here represented. If we suppose, to throw light on the

[3] *Ancient Beliefs and Modern Superstitions*, pp. 66–7.

[4] St Matthew xx, 1–16.

[5] Ibid. xix, 30.

question, that there are two spiritual men more or less equally gifted, and that one of them is condemned to die the next day, whereas no such sentence hangs over the other, it is not difficult to see that the condemned man is in ideal circumstances for realizing, immediately and profoundly, a total commitment to the things of the Afterlife, and that he thereby has a certain priority over the other man. Not that we now living are in ourselves any more condemned that our ancestors were; but in their day the macrocosm itself was not under sentence of imminent 'death', as now it is; and this imminence engenders a climate which is potentially favourable to otherworldliness, and which can be made to serve spiritual ends as it were by refraction from macrocosm to microcosm. The climate of the eleventh hour can also be favourable to spiritual fruition and fulfilment in the same incalculable and mysterious way.

A third reason why the last should be first is related to what might be called spiritual impetus. The parable's esoteric context makes all the more obvious the symbolism of the vineyard and also, by contrast, of the marketplace from which the labourers were hired. The fact that they were 'standing idle in the marketplace' may be taken as a sign of their virtual spirituality. To be busy in the marketplace and thus fully identified with it is to be, like the rich young man, passive towards the pull of the outer world. The parable thus serves to reiterate also, by implication, what is—and has been throughout historic times[6]—the great choice with which mankind is faced, the choice between 'vineyard' and 'marketplace', that is, between being active with regard to the Kingdom of Heaven and remaining passive in outward profanity. But if the vineyard is a prolongation of the Kingdom,[7] the marketplace was always, in every civilization except the modern one, a prolon-

[6] This reservation is necessary because there must have been a time when the 'marketplace', even in its most positive sense, namely exoterism, did not yet exist.

[7] The parable begins: 'The kingdom of heaven is like unto a man that is an householder, which went out early in the morning to hire labourers unto his vineyard.'

gation of the vineyard. The passage from one to the other was relatively easy, the way was clearly signposted, the immense superiority of the vineyard was officially recognized in the marketplace which was even, to a certain extent, a preparation for it. But today there is no connection whatsoever between the two, and the dominant ideas of the one are at the opposite pole from those of the other. The passage from marketplace to vineyard now requires, in addition to the qualifications which have always been necessary, a penetration and a resolution capable of making a break with one's past more totally than ever before; and the liberating efforts of intelligence and will that are thus called into action may be prolonged, after the vineyard has been reached, to add their momentum, combined with that of the eleventh hour itself,[8] to the 'work', that is, to the spiritual path.

There is yet another reason, no doubt the most powerful of all, why the last should be first, and we will come back to it later. Meantime it is relevant to mention a sign yet to be realized in which there lies, for mankind, a grave responsibility. This herald of the end, which is none the less distinct from the end, is the devastation of which it was said: 'And except those days should be shortened, there should no flesh be saved: but for the elect's sake those days shall be shortened.'[9] To speak of an elect is to speak of the 'vineyard'; and it is assuredly not this precinct but 'the marketplace'—the modern civilization—which is to be destroyed. Elsewhere[10] the days are referred to as 'the days of vengeance',[11] and

[8] It is a mistake to suppose that the flow of time is uniform; in earlier ages the temporal condition lies more lightly on the world, as it does on the young in the analogous lesser cycle of human life; but as the cycle advances time tightens its grip which means that it makes itself felt as an ever increasing impetus, whence the 'velocity' to which mankind is now subjected, and which can become a spiritual advantage wherever life has been made to flow in a spiritual channel.

[9] St Matthew, xxiv, 22.

[10] St Luke, xxi, 22.

[11] The auditions referred to in what follows are clearly relevant, and they deserve our attention in virtue of the person who experienced them. In 1957 Pope Pius xii authorized the process of beatification of Francisco and Jacinta, two shepherd children to whom the

since Providence is by definition long-suffering, the immanence of an overflow of Divine Anger proves that a limit has been reached, and that a sector of the human race has gone to certain negative extremes. It is these above all which make it now imperative for a would-be worker in the 'vineyard' to turn his back on the 'marketplace' more implacably than ever before. But in order to do so it is necessary to see the modern world's enormities as such, and to be actively and vigilantly opposed to them, instead of being, if only subconsciously, their passive accomplice. With this in view, the next two chapters are, in their different ways, a demonstration of some of the extremes in question.

Blessed Virgin had appeared several times at Fatima in Portugal in 1917. This papal decision meant that a prominent member of the commission concerned with the process had to make an official visit to Sister Lucia, the third visionary of Fatima—now a nun in the Carmelite Convent at Coimbra—to interrogate her about the last days of her two fellow seers; and amongst what was published later, apart from what concerned the immediate purpose of the interview, there were certain general remarks made by Sister Lucia of which we may quote the following: 'Three times Our Lady has told me that we are approaching the latter days . . . The Lord will punish the world very soon . . . Many nations will vanish from the face of the earth.'

3

'And from him that hath not . . .'

THERE ARE beyond doubt many in the world of today, perhaps even a majority, who would be inclined to put the question: 'What it is about our times rather than any other which has brought "the cup of God's anger"[1] to the brink of overflow?' Not that anyone considers these times to be perfect, or even good; but modern education tends to inculcate the conviction that previous centuries were considerably less good, and that the further back we go, the worse the world becomes. Yet none of the people of those 'dark ages' would have presumed to ask the above question. On the contrary they felt, mistakenly in fact, that they had indeed reached an extreme of guilt such as might well bring down on them the Divine vengeance. That the question 'Why on us?' should be asked today by a majority is not only a sign of the times but one could also say that the very putting of the question is itself the answer to the question. In other words, modern man's lack of sense of his own shortcoming is crucial; and this lack is not to be separated from its cause, namely, the failure to understand the true nature of man. If that nature were understood, the ideal it represents would serve as a criterion in the light of which

[1] In the last of her apparitions to the four peasant girls at Garabandal in Spain between the years 1961 and 1965, the Blessed Virgin said: 'previously the cup was filling; now it is almost overflowing'. From the context it is clear that the reference is to the cup of Divine Anger. (See F. Sanchez-Ventura y Pascual, *The Apparitions of Garabandal*, pp. 171–3.)

the past would appear much less bad and the present much less good.

There is no traditional divergence, from one end of the world to the other, as to what constitutes primordial man, and the same applies to fallen man. The imagery used to tell of the Fall may differ from religion to religion, but the loss incurred is always the same, that is, loss of centrality and therefore of contact with the vertical axis which connects this state with all the higher states. 'Original sin' is nothing other than the incapacity, by reason of that loss, to be what the Taoists call 'True Man', that is, to fulfil adequately man's primordial function of Pontifex, of 'bridge-maker' or mediator between this world and all that lies above it. But the privation incurred at the Fall was not absolute, nor has man been replaced as mediator by any other creature. There is therefore still only one criterion for judging the worth of any human individual, and that is his nearness—or farness—with regard to the centre, and the intensity—or laxity—of his aspiration to transcend his fallen state.

In answer to this chapter's initial question, it would be possible—though it would not be the best answer—to draw up an almost endless list of twentieth-century facts which reverberate with evidence that man has reached a limit of distance from his primordial nature. Yet to list factual examples would be merely to lay hands on the fringe of the question. Incomparably more significant is the general attitude and outlook of which the examples are the excrescences.

It may be argued that generations other than the more recent ones have fallen far short of the human norm, and this no one could rightly deny. But modern man is unique in having fallen so far as to lose sight of it, to the point of questioning its existence, and even of fabricating a new 'norm' out of the limitations of his own decadent experience. Our less recent ancestors knew that they had 'come down from above'; twentieth-century man is alone in thinking and in priding himself that he has 'come up from below'.

The basic purpose of religion is to open up, for man, the way of return to his lost centrality. So long as he possessed spontaneously his bond with the Transcendent, the 'ligament' to which the term *religio* refers, it was not necessary for Heaven to reveal a religion in the ordinary sense. The first revealed religion was the response of Providence to the Fall of man, and this Divine redress established on earth a Golden Age, named in Sanskrit *Krita-Yuga* because in it the rites necessary for regaining what was lost were 'accomplished'. Thus, by religion, the world of man became once more, albeit at a lower level than that of the Terrestrial Paradise, an image of Perfection. Every image of the Absolute is, however, bound ultimately to confess that it is merely an image,[2] and that first age could not retain the level of its outset. The continuance of religion, when endangered, was ensured by further Divine Revelations,[3] subsequent to that which inaugurated the Golden Age. It was thus made always possible for the downward impetus to be checked for many individuals and for some, an ever decreasing number, to be overcome altogether. But the impetus is bound to continue as a general tendency down to the end of the cycle

[2] This applies to all that is relative, even the Heavens. But these worlds of the Spirit, although created, are the domain of inviolability, for they are as it were plunged in the Light of the 'Divine Halo'. The Paradise of the Essence, from which this Light emanates, is the Absolute Itself; and into Its Infinite Perfection the created universe is ultimately reabsorbed. It is by this reabsorption—the Apocatastasis—that the Celestial Paradises avow their relativity, and they do so within the framework of the safety, immortality and incorruptibility that Salvation guarantees. 'The Paradises, at the approach of the Apocatastasis, will of metaphysical necessity reveal their limitative aspect, as if they had become less vast or as if God were less close than before . . . Without involving suffering of any kind, which would be contrary to the very definition of Heaven, the aspect "other than God" will manifest itself to the detriment of the aspect "near to God". This will be no more than a passing shadow, for then will come the Apocatastasis whose glory will surpass all promises and all expectations in conformity with the principle that God never fulfils less than He promises, but on the contrary always more.' (Frithjof Schuon, *Dimensions of Islam*, p. 137.)

[3] The spiritual path, that is, the path of return to the centre, is also in a sense a chain of losses and restorations of equilibrium. But there it is always a question of sacrificing a lower equilibrium in order to gain a higher one, whereas in the unfolding of the cycle of manifestation it is the inverse that takes place.

when the world as a whole reaches its maximum 'separation' from its Divine Origin.

The outlook that governs the modern civilization and that characterizes anyone who would be generally recognized as a 'typical product of the twentieth century' may be considered as a negative extreme in that it represents no less than man's capitulation to the exact opposite of truth as regards what concerns him most, that is, the nature and function of the human being—a capitulation that is all the more total for being unconscious. That is indeed the crux of the matter, for instead of being bent on regaining what was lost, the loser has come to believe that he has suffered no loss whatsoever, and that mankind, having evolved from next to nothing, is now better than it has ever been. There are even some so-called religious authorities who would like to abolish the dogma of original sin on the grounds that it is an insult to the dignity of the fully developed and enlightened *homo sapiens* of today.

So total a defection would have seemed impossible, even in a relatively near past. But the parable of the talents explains how the apparently impossible can be realised in a downward as well as in an upward direction. For just as the spiritual path, that is, the path of excelling oneself, is only practicable because 'unto every one that hath shall be given, and he shall have abundance', so also, because 'from him that hath not shall be taken away even that which he hath',[4] the unspiritual man is liable to find himself suddenly lacking in those very endowments that seemed most securely his. Thus, for example, the rationalist and the modern scientist, having closed themselves to the Spirit by demanding rational and scientific explanations of transcendent truths, are liable to find themselves deserted by logic and by science in the hour of greatest need. Still bristling with anti-religious arguments, they have meekly let themselves become dupes of one of

[4] St Matthew, xxv, 29.

the most subrational persuasions and one of the most unscientific theories that have ever trespassed upon the mind of man.

Though in many respects they overlap, rationalism and scientism may be considered as the two poles, subjective and objective, of the pseudo-religion of the modern world. Rationalism, with its false logic, wishful thinking, and warped sense of values supplies the pseudo-faith, namely, the belief that man has progressed throughout the ages and that he will inevitably continue to progress in the future. The error here is almost entirely subjective: progressism is rooted in complacency, and it depends not so much on false data as on a false interpretation of certain facts. In scientism, which supplies the pseudo-doctrine of evolution, the error is mainly objective, at any rate as far as the 'layman' is concerned. Here the scientist, who is the 'high priest' of the modern world and who alone has the power to speak *ex cathedra*, misleads his flock with a false object of faith. This is by far the greatest stumbling block, for the question of progress must always remain a matter of opinion, but evolution is presented as a scientific fact that 'transcends' all discussion; and whereas truly transcendent doctrines lend wings to the intelligence, the pseudo-transcendent paralyses it and sets up a stifling 'dictatorship' in the soul.

As to the 'layman', it must be admitted that he is subject to a considerable pressure. He is pounded by a battery of scientific terms he does not understand, and on the face of it there would seem to be no reason why the scientist—dry, matter-of-fact, purely objective, and infallibly accurate, as he is supposed to be—should wish to deceive as regards evolution. The public is not to know that the scientist is evolutionist, not in virtue of his science, but by 'religion'; yet though this secret is not always well kept,[5] the victims

[5] Some evolutionists make it very clear in their writings and broadcast talks that their case is an outstanding illustration of the truth that man is nothing if not religious, and that if he gives up his religion he inevitably transfers his religious sentiments to something else, endowing it with all those rights and privileges that are the due of religion alone.

of the deception are for the most part only too eager to be deceived. Progressism is, for evolutionism, the most fertile of soils.

In this context the theories of evolution and progress may be likened to the two cards that are placed one against the other at the 'foundation' of a card house. If they did not support each other, both would fall flat, and the whole edifice, that is the outlook that dominates the modern world, would collapse. The idea of evolution would have been accepted neither by scientists nor by 'laymen' if the nineteenth-century European had not been convinced of progress in the face of all appearances to the contrary. To those who refuse to see these appearances and who continue to believe in progress 'because of all that man has achieved in the last hundred years' and 'because there is such promise for the future', there is clearly nothing to be said. But for those whose progressism is propped up only by evolutionism and leans with all its weight on the teaching that evolution is 'a scientifically proved fact', it can be a relief comparable to waking up after a bad dream to read an objective assessment of evolutionism by a scientist who is not an evolutionist. One such assessment is Douglas Dewar's book *The Transformist Illusion.*[6] Another is Evan Shute's *Flaws in the Theory of Evolution.*[7]

Shute's title is an understatement, for his book is a demonstration that the theory in question is pure conjecture: the only evolution that has been scientifically attested is on a very small scale and within narrow limits. To conclude from this 'micro-evolution', which no one contests, that there could be such a thing as 'mega-evolution'—for example, that the class of birds could have evolved from the class of reptiles—is not merely conjecture but perverse conjecture, for as Shute points out, micro-evolution demonstrates the presence in nature of all sorts of unseen barriers that ensure the stability of the various classes and orders of animals and plants and that invariably cause transformation, when it has run its little course, to come to a dead end.

[6] Sophia Perennis, 1995. [7] Craig Press, Nutley, NJ, 1961.

The realm of conjecture is always the realm of disagreement. Moreover some evolutionists are more scientific than others, and when their sense of science has been outraged beyond measure, they have not always been able to resist pouring scorn on some of the more fantastic ideas of their fellow evolutionists. As a rule such sallies are isolated and have little effect, if indeed they do not pass unnoticed, but when gathered together, as they are in *Flaws in the Theory of Evolution*, their weight is considerable; and by quoting from the evolutionists themselves,[8] Shute has been able to show that the theory of mega-evolution is no more than a shell inside which its champions have demolished each other's conjectures until there is nothing left.

To sum up his thesis, the more science delves into the amazing intricacies of nature, the more overwhelming is the evidence that piles up against evolutionism. As he himself puts it: 'Mega-evolution is really a philosophy dating from the days of biological ignorance; it was a philosophic synthesis built up in a biological kindergarten.'

Dewar, in his book, gives amongst other things many outrageous examples of the way in which evolutionist texts continually rely on the ignorance or inobservance of the 'layman'. From these examples we will quote a remark of Darwin's which is of basic significance: 'With some savages the foot has not altogether lost its prehensile power, as is shown by their manner of climbing trees, and of using them in other ways.' The truth is, as Darwin must have known, that any human being can develop with practice, if driven by circumstances, certain powers of grasping with the feet. But such development can be only within very narrow limits, for organically the human foot, unlike the human hand, is not made for grasping. It is made to serve as a basis for

[8] By way of example, he quotes from the American palaeontologist Professor E. A. Hooton: 'You can, with equal facility, model on a Neanderthaloid skull the features of a chimpanzee or the lineaments of a philosopher. These alleged restorations of ancient types of man have very little, if any, scientific value, and are likely only to mislead the public.'

man's upright posture and gait, whereas the 'foot' of an ape is organically as prehensile as a hand. In the human foot the transverse ligament binds together all five toes whereas in the ape it leaves the big toe free like a thumb. Let every reader now look at his own hand, which in the above respect is similar to the foot of an ape, and ask himself whether it is imaginable that even in millions of millions of years the ligament that binds together the four fingers could ever come to throw out a kind of noose, lassoo the thumb, and bind it up together with the fingers, all this, presumably, taking place under the skin. When Darwin says, 'the foot has not altogether lost its prehensile power', does he mean 'the lassooing has already taken place but the roping in has not quite been effected'? But he relies on such questions not being asked.

Looking at evolutionism from quite a different angle—one that is closer to that of our main theme—it must be remembered that only by escaping from time can man escape from the phases of time. The spiritual path escapes from these phases because only its starting point lies within time. From there onward it is a 'vertical' upward movement through supratemporal domains as represented in Dante's *Purgatorio* and *Paradiso*. But modern science does not know of any such possibility of an escape from the temporal condition. The gradual ascent of no return that the evolutionist has in mind is an idea that has been surreptitiously borrowed from religion and naively transferred from the supratemporal to the temporal. In entertaining such an idea he is turning his back on his own scientific principles. Every process of development known to modern science is subject to a waxing and waning analogous to the phases of man's life. Even civilizations, as history can testify, have their dawn, their noon, their late afternoon, and their twilight. If the evolutionist outlook were genuinely 'scientist', in the modern sense, it would be assumed that the evolution of the human race was a phase of waxing that would necessarily be followed by the complementary waning phase of devolution; and the question of whether or not man was already on the downward phase would be a major feature of all evolutionist literature. The fact that the question is never put, and that if evolutionists could be made to face up to it most of them would drop their theory as one drops a hot coal, does not say much for their objectivity.

There could be no such question of any such evolution from the standpoint of ancient science, which did not claim to have everything within it scope, that is, within the temporal domain. It could therefore admit to being transcended by the origins of earthly things. For these origins it looked beyond temporal duration to the Divine creative act that places man (and the whole earthly state) on a summit from which there can only be a decline. The same applies to the different religions, which also have their origins outside time, not in the sense that their respective starting points cannot be more or less dated, but in virtue of each religion's essential aspect, the supratemporal 'ligament' which binds it to the Eternal and without which it could have no efficacy, and also in virtue of the spirituality of its founder who is likewise rooted in Eternity. But this does not apply to the theocratic civilization which is non-existent at the outset of a religion, from which it has to grow in time and therefore, as we have just seen, to wax and then wane.[9]

It is in the final phase of a cycle that a world reaches its extremity of separation from the Principle. Such a period is one of 'remoteness' from God, and one of its necessary characteristics is a humanity largely made up of men and women who have no conception of man's true nature and responsibility. He is for them, not the representative of God on earth, but merely the summit of the animal kingdom. With their backs turned to the centre that is man's rightful place as mediator between Heaven

[9] We will come back later to this somewhat complex question to which I have already devoted a chapter, 'The Rhythms of Time', in *Ancient Beliefs and Modern Superstitions* (Archetype, Cambridge, 2001).

and earth, their 'orientation' is entirely outward, in the direction of the boundary that separates humanity from the lower orders. The centrifugal tendency of modern man is often written on his face so clearly that if an evolutionist were at the same time something of a physiognomist[10] he would indeed see reason to suppose that mankind, having reached its highest point of evolution, was already well advanced in the complementary phase of devolution.

Although such a supposition would bring him, as we shall see, far nearer the truth than he is now, he would none the less be wrong to suppose that the dividing line that separates humanity from the lower orders, as far as life on earth is concerned, could be crossed by anything but a miraculous suspension of the laws of nature. Sacred texts tell us of men having been transformed into apes by an overflow of Divine Anger, but mankind could never, by any natural course, devolve into apekind any more than the reverse process could take place. Such transformations would require organic changes that, miracles apart, could be effected only by drastic surgical operations. But a man can, after death, 'become an ape' in the sense that he can pass on into another state of existence in which, having lost his centrality, he might occupy a position analogous to that of an ape in this world; and an ape could 'become man' in the sense that through some mysterious

[10] An unlikely combination, for physiognomy presupposes the knowledge of what man is and, above all, what God is. The Prophet of Islam said: 'When anyone of you strikes a blow (in battle) let him avoid striking the face (of his enemy), for God created Adam in His image'. This somewhat elliptical utterance demands, by way of commentary, the addition: '. . . and it is in the face that the image is especially concentrated'. The human face is a mirror that reflects the Divine Qualities. The human hand is also such a mirror, but to be read, it requires knowledge of a special science, whereas the face is an open book to be read by effortless intuition; and physiognomy is nothing other than the ability to see, in any given face, how full and direct (or as the case may be, how fragmentary and oblique) the reflection is. Traditionally, physiognomical powers are associated with faith (the Prophet said: 'Beware the believer's power to read the face'), and in fact the man best qualified to judge the quality of a mirror, that is, to judge how faithfully it mirrors an object, is the man who has the clearest vision of that object in itself, apart from the mirror.

working of Divine Grace[11] he might, after his death in this world, be born at the centre of the world that comes 'next' to it on the rim of the *samsara*, the great wheel of universal existence.

It is the function of religion, or one of its functions to convey to man as much knowledge as he can assimilate with profit; religions differ in exactly what they convey and what they withhold because of the differences of human collectivities. The scope of this book clearly will not allow us to dwell on the question at any length, but it may be remarked in passing that the doctrine of the *samsara*, which was not unknown to pre-Christian Europe but which is no more than implicit in Semitic monotheism, has become once more accessible to the Western world from Hinduism and Buddhism—accessible, that is, to anyone who feels impelled to make a serious study of religion.

According to this doctrine, our present state of earthly existence is merely one of a seemingly endless series of analogous states, all at the same untranscendent level, which we might call sub-spiritual or subcelestial. Each of these successive worlds has, at its centre, a 'narrow gate' which opens onto the Transcendent and which is a way of escape from the chain of samsaric rebirths and redeaths. But the ascendant aspiration needed for this deliverance is given to none but the central species of each state, that is, man and his counterparts in the other worlds. Peripheral creatures are not free to take any initiative for their own advancement. Although, as we have seen, it is not impossible for them to be reborn into a central state, they cannot actively[12] co-operate with

[11] Generally speaking, the most desirable destiny in this life for a peripheral being is to be intimately associated with a man who fulfils his centrality enough to be, in some degree, Pontifex. It is also as Pontifex that a man ritually sacrifices an animal. As to ascents made at lower levels in the hierarchy, from one peripheral degree to another, it cannot be inauspicious for a lower being to be overwhelmed and absorbed by a higher one. The law of the jungle would seem to be woven upon the hidden mercies of such evolutions.

[12] But passively, they are able to submit to the powerful attraction that spirituality can have for them—witness the remarkable relationships which have existed between Saints and animals and of which examples are to be found in the hagiographies of all the religions.

the workings of Divine Grace on their behalf. But a central being can and must co-operate: failure to do so, that is, failure to follow the guidance offered by religion, means deviation from centrality, by outwardness or, at the worst, by downwardness. This greater offence would mean, at death, a descent into one of the samsaric hells, whereas the lesser offence of outwardness would entail, as its natural consequence, the loss of inwardness or centrality, that is, rebirth into the next world as something analogous to one of the peripheral creatures of this world.

The reasons are obvious why the later religions have concentrated on our world to the exclusion of its innumerable counterparts. To escape from one world is to escape from them all; and 'sufficient unto the day is the evil thereof', which might be interpreted 'sufficient unto one world is the evil thereof', its evil being, all told, the difficulty of escape from it. But truth has its rights, and nothing less than the full doctrine of the *samsara* is capable of giving a concept of the universe adequate to what the contemplative intelligence demands[13] as a symbolic basis for meditating on the Divine Infinitude. Moreover the universe, for all its multiplicity, is one whole, so that any simplification of cosmology is liable to leave certain loose threads hanging, to the detriment of any religion that cannot tie them into place.

In the past the majority of people found it natural that not everything should be explained to them. They were satisfied with the promises of religion that what was left unaccounted for in this life would be fully clarified in the Hereafter. But today the danger

[13] This doctrine has therefore, in the nature of things, found its way into monotheistic esoterism. Jalāl ad-Dīn ar-Rūmī, the great Persian Sufi of the thirteenth century, speaks of pre-human peripheral states and of rebirth from mineral to vegetable, from vegetable to animal and from animal to man (*Mathnavi*, III, 3901 *et seq.*, and IV, 3637 *et seq.*, in Nicholson's translation pp. 218 and 472.) Some have interpreted these lines as evolutionism—falsely because there is no gradual development but a series of sudden transformations, and above all because the mineral, vegetable, animal and human states are envisaged as already existing and fully developed. The evolution in question is that of a single being, from the lowest to the highest of these states, from the periphery to the centre.

of 'loose threads' is considerable owing to the existence of so many overactive minds 'set free', as they would put it, 'from the shackles of religion', and enthusiastically bent on sharing their emancipation with others. These 'liberators' are not slow to seize upon certain aspects of our times which the monotheistic perspective has not accounted for and which seem to be incompatible with reliance upon Divine Justice and therefore with belief in God.

If beings have had no existence previous to this life, how can we explain the birth of thousands of souls day after day into conditions spiritually so unfavourable as to offer no apparent hope of salvation? But if one is aware that our position in this state was 'earned' in our previous state upon the great round of existences, the problem no longer looms so large. The state of those countless people in the modern world who do not seem to have been given 'a fair chance' can only be the result of their having already developed a centrifugal impetus in one of the *samsara*'s other worlds. The people in question are born into this world at the outside edge of humanity because they had already, in their pre-terrestrial state, deliberately turned a blind eye to the obligations with which centrality is fraught.

If the cosmologies and eschatologies of the more ancient religions have become to a certain extent necessary, they are none the less too vast for the non-contemplative majority of the end of the Iron Age. For most of those who hear it, the doctrine of *samsara* is doomed in advance to lead to the illusion of reincarnationism,[14] that is, belief in a series of rebirths into this world, for it is difficult to speak of the other worlds except in terms of the

[14] Reincarnation is often wrongly thought to have been proved by metempsychosis, the transference of certain characteristics from one individual, at his death, to another. Probably the best known examples of metempsychosis are those which have made it possible, after the death of a Dalai Lama, to identify his heir. But there is no question here of the older man's reincarnation in the younger man, nor is it possible for a being to pass twice through the same samsaric world. See, in this connection, Whitall N. Perry, *Challenges to a Secular Society*, The Foundation for Traditional Studies, 1998.

one world we know. But dangers of this illusion can be obviated by a true sense of values. The statement that a man could be born in his next life as a lower animal or even as a vegetable or a mineral conveys adequately a truth, provided that the imagination of the hearer is keen enough to galvanize him into the determination to make the most of the inestimable privilege of a central state, 'so hard to obtain'.[15] The danger of the doctrine, apart from the distractions that it may lead to, is always that an unimaginative wishful thinker will abstract from it the notion that he will be given 'another chance' and turn a blind eye to all the rest. But this danger is as nothing compared with the danger of believing that there is no life of any kind after death, a danger that hangs like a shadow over every child who is born into all but the most traditional parts of the modern world.

In any case, the error of reincarnationism cannot be put on a level with the error of evolutionism. The word 'reincarnation' as currently used expresses metaphorically, if not literally, what does actually take place. But evolutionism together with its inseparable complement of progressism, is nothing but a parody of the spiritual path of escape from the *samsara*, a parody that flattens the vertical to the horizontal and for having 'played one's part' offers as a prize to be awarded posthumously or more precisely 'humously'—that is, not to a blessed spirit but to a corpse—an ever-receding earthly 'welfare' of doubtful possibility and doubtful desirability.

Let us now consider, with special reference to religion and in particular to Christianity, the part played by education in the modern Western world. Generally speaking, and always allowing for exceptions, it would be true to say that in most of their lessons, partly through what they are taught and partly owing to the general outlook that all too clearly prevails among the teachers, the pupils are indoctrinated with the modern pseudo-religion; and in the hour or two a week set aside for the study of the Bible

15 See Marco Pallis, *A Buddhist Spectrum*, chapter IV.

they are given a glimpse of an opposite perspective, though the contradictions are presented as 'tactfully' as possible, always at the expense of religion. In some cases the first chapters of Genesis are omitted; in others they are taught without comment; in others they are taught as 'myths' in the modern ignoble misuse of that noble word. The pupils' attention is for the most part unlikely to be drawn to the fact that Christianity has some of its deepest roots in these very chapters, to the point that if they are false, then so is it. But a little reflection will bring this out; nor does religion, lukewarmly, fragmentarily, apologetically presented as it is, stand much chance when the pupils are faced with a serious choice between it and modernism. The result is that those who cling to their already precarious faith instinctively block their own channels of spiritual thought, and by a kind of self-imposed mental paralysis, scarcely daring to think about their religion, they sacrifice a vital aspect of sincerity as defined by Christ in his first commandment: 'Thou shalt love the Lord thy God . . . with all thy mind'; and it is precisely this part of the commandment that depends most on our human initiative, the part that we should be best able, by our own efforts, to fulfil, though the question of grace can never be absent.

An eminent prisoner within this framework of mental paralysis is Teilhard de Chardin, who also blocks the main and obvious channels of thought in his desperate attempts to combine religion with evolutionism. His appeal lies in his providing certain ingeniously devised side channels which relieve the paralytic by keeping up an illusion of normal mental activity. In other words, with an extraordinary capacity for turning a blind eye and a deaf ear to this and that, he creates a kind of mental hubbub in order to drown the voice or reason, refusing altogether to put himself the following questions which, for anyone who has received a modern Western education, loudly cry out to be asked:

If God exists, as we are taught to believe, and if evolution is a scientific fact, as we are forbidden doubt, what sort of being can

God be? Why did He choose to turn mankind back towards the past in longing for a lost Paradise, and to leave them so turned, in all parts of the world, for thousands of years, if He knew that the truth lay in just the opposite direction? Why could He not have taught them about evolution to begin with? Or at least brought them gradually to it, instead of allowing religion after religion to repeat and confirm the same old way of thinking? And why did He allow this to culminate, at any rate for the Western world, in a religion that perhaps more inextricably than any other is bound up with the doctrine of the Fall of man?[16] And why, having prevented all His prophets from divulging evolution, did He allow a mere layman to stumble upon it and to propagate it in defiance of all spiritual authorities of the day, thereby causing millions of people to lose their faith in religion and in Him?

'God moves in a mysterious way', some will argue, in a frantic attempt to retain both God and evolutionism. But you cannot sew up a gaping chasm with such a needle and thread. Seek to retain these two incompatibilities, and you will be left with a deity who is not the Lord of All Mystery but a subhuman monster of incompetence, which is precisely what Teilhardism implies of God.[17] But outside the very special climate of this pseudomystical fantasy, one only needs to be able to put two and two together to see that either evolutionism or God must go; and modern education begins to tip the scale in favour of evolutionism at an increasingly early age.

[16] Islam is just as explicit about the Fall as Christianity is, but unlike Christianity it is not centred on any historical redeeming sacrifice in view of the Fall.

[17] This escapes the notice of Teilhardists because they are not really interested in God. Neither was Teilhard de Chardin himself, as he makes clear in the following confession: 'If in consequence of some inner subversion, I should lose successively my faith in Christ, my faith in a personal god, my faith in the Spirit, it seems to me that I would continue to believe in the world. The world—the value, the infallibility and the goodness of the world—this is, in the last analysis, the first and only thing in which I believe.' See Kurt Almquist, 'Aspects of Teilhardian Idolatry', in *Studies in Comparative Religion*, Summer-Autumn, 1978. See also Wolfgang Smith, *Teilhardism and the New Religion* and my review of it in *Sophia*, Summer, 1997.

'First of all Copernicus, and the discovery that the earth moves round the sun; then Darwin, and the discovery that men have evolved from apes.' Such is the train of thought which is encouraged to prevail. It is never pointed out that the implicit logic is false, that there is no comparison between the two men in question, and that their respective theories did not even result from the same process of thought, inasmuch as Darwin's theory is pure hypothesis. This last fact is in any case unknown to most of the teachers, who in their own youth were misled as they now mislead. So the seemingly unanswerable and conclusive argument of the two discoveries is left unquestioned,[18] to seep into the souls of the young and to eliminate there all respect for tradition, while 'proving' the validity of modern scepticism. It is therefore not surprising that many Westerners, even before they have left school, have already opted, if not for atheism, at least for an agnostic reserve of judgement that they, like their parents, will probably never see fit to unreserve. But a normally functioning mind, which is just what they are systematically deprived of—that is, a mind neither warped by rationalism nor spellbound by materialist scientism—would have no difficulty, when faced by the above questions, in finding the right answer and in razing the 'card house' of modern ideology to the ground.

'What then,' it may be asked, 'should we teach?' The answer is: as far as possible the whole truth, which would mean teaching many truths which were not taught in better times, for the needs of the eleventh hour are not the same as those of the sixth or seventh. By way of example, let the young be taught, towards the end of their schooling, that many scientists have conjectured—but in no sense proved—that mankind has evolved from a lower

[18] If questioned at all, the argument dissolves into nothing, for the one discovery worthy of the name, that of Copernicus, was more in the nature of a rediscovery, since there is reason to suppose that the fact in question was known to some of the ancients. None the less, it is also a cosmological fact that the sun appears to go round the earth, and the human race will no doubt continue to speak of sunrise and sunset for as long as the world exists.

species. This conjecture is an incident in the history of our day. But let them be taught at the same time that the theory in question, which has only crossed the mind of man in relatively recent years, is the exact opposite not merely of what the Bible teaches us but also of the unanimous opinion of the whole pre-Biblical world in all parts of the globe. In particular, the tradition of the four ages of the temporal cycle, Golden, Silver, Bronze and Iron, which dominated the perspective of classical antiquity, going back into the shadows of prehistory, has also been prevalent from equally ancient times among the Hindus and the American Indians.[19] Or to take one aspect of the evolutionary conjecture, namely that human language evolved from the inarticulate sounds of animals, let it be pointed out that although the origin of language is beyond investigation, linguistic science can none the less take us back to a very remote past, and it teaches us that the oldest languages are the most complex and majestic, while being also the richest in variety of consonantal sounds. All languages in use today have devolved from more elaborate languages which they have simplified and in general mutilated and corrupted. Devolution, not evolution, is also the fate of many word meanings. All students should be made to study the already mentioned degradation of the word 'intellect'. It is a scientific fact that throughout the ancient world the concept of man's faculties was more exalted and of wider scope that it is today.

Let the traditional and the modern concepts of the universe—or, if one prefers it, of reality—be placed side by side. According to typically modern thought, 'reality' is supposed to have originally consisted of the material world alone. It is said that life must have been 'sparked off', in some as yet unexplained way, from matter, and that living organisms developed psychic faculties, first of all the senses, then sentiment and memory, and then, as man himself gradually evolved, imagination and reason. According to the traditional explanation, on the other hand it is not the higher

[19] Joseph E. Brown, *The Sacred Pipe*, p.9.

which proceeds from the lower but the lower from the higher; nor is existence limited to the psychic and the corporeal. The Supreme Origin—and End—of all things is Absolute Truth, which alone has Reality in the full sense, and which manifests or creates, at lesser degrees of reality, the whole of existence.[20] The traditional theory of existence, common to all religions, is summed up in the Islamic holy[21] tradition: 'I was a Hidden Treasure, and I loved to be known, and so I created the world.' The psychic and the corporeal, soul and body, are the two lowest levels of reality, and together they constitute what we call 'this world'. Above them is the domain of the Spirit, known as 'the next world' from the standpoint of life on earth, but first in order of creation, for it is no less than the primal 'overflow' of the Divine Reality Itself. From that immediate reflection of the Hidden Treasure, the psychic domain is a projected image which in its turn projects the bodily domain.

The language of symbolism, which is part of man's primordial heritage, is based on this hierarchy of the different degrees of the universe. A symbol is not something arbitrarily chosen by man to illustrate a higher reality; it does so precisely because it is rooted in that reality, which has projected it, like a shadow or a reflection, onto the plane of earth. Every terrestrial object is the outcome of a series of projections, from Divine to spiritual, from spiritual to psychic, from psychic to corporeal. But on this lowest plane which is the remotest of all from the Divine Archetypes, and which, being deployed in time and in space, undergoes an extremity of differentiation and fragmentation, it is necessary to distinguish between peripheral objects that are no more than faint and fragmentary reflections and the more central objects of each domain,

[20] The etymological sense of this word, from *ex* + *sistere*, 'to stand out from' is relevant to our context, for which existence is distinct from Being. God Alone is; from His Being existence proceeds and is ultimately reintegrated into It.

[21] So called because in it the Divinity speaks in the first person on the tongue of the Prophet.

that is, of each subdivision of the animal, vegetable and mineral kingdoms. The term symbol is reserved for those most direct manifestations which reflect their archetypes with the greatest clarity and which thus have the power to bring about a 'remembrance', in the Platonic sense, of the transcendent truth that is symbolized.

In every domain there are orders of precedence which are still felt but no longer, for the most part, understood. The criterion of an object's rank is its symbolic value. By way of example, gold takes precedence over other metals, just as amongst stones the diamond, the ruby, the sapphire and the emerald rank highest, and all these are powerfully symbolic. In a different domain, the same can be said of such insects as the bee, the butterfly and the spider. In particular the symbolism of the spider is very relevant to our context, for it would be incapable of weaving its web from its own substance if creation were not woven out of the substance of the Creator. Nor could the web take the form of concentric circles in ever receding distance from the centre if the Divine Creative Act did not project the planes of existence in a hierarchy of degrees, each subsequent plane being more remote from its Divine Origin. Nor again could the spider have its centrality and almost at the same time the agile omnipresence which gives it a comprehensive authority over the web if the Infinite and Eternal Truth were not mysteriously both Centre and Encompasser of all creation. In this connection we may refer back to the already mentioned rediscovery made by Copernicus, for the metaphysical reconciliation between geocentrism and heliocentrism is closely related to the two Divine Aspects we have just spoken of. On the plane of this world, both man and the sun are outstanding as manifestations or reflections of the Divinity, who is represented as Centre by the factual centrality of the sun and as Encompasser by the sun's phenomenal orbit round the earth. Inversely, in the case of man, the Divine Centre is symbolized by his phenomenal centrality, whereas the factual orbit of man's earth round the sun is an image of the

Divine Encompassing. Considered in this way, both the ignorance of the geocentrists and the enlightenment of the heliocentrists appear to be less absolute than they are often made out to be.

Without the knowledge of the basic traditional concepts which are the theme of these last paragraphs it is impossible to understand ancient thought and therefore, amongst other things, sacred art, which speaks the language of symbolism. Moreover it may be noticed that without the doctrine of the different degrees of universal existence, a whole section of words—not only intellect—becomes unusable, at any rate according to the meanings which alone justify their existence. Specifically modern thought, which refuses to believe that there is anything above the psychic level, thereby denies itself the right to such words as 'metaphysical' and 'transcendent'. Even the word 'wisdom' is in jeopardy—or would be if it were not possible to qualify it with the epithet 'worldly'—for without the sense of hierarchy and a knowledge of metaphysical truths there could not even be the first glimmerings of what our remote ancestors understood by 'wisdom'.

Once the exact relationship between science and evolutionism has been established, and once the traditional doctrine of creation has been explained in a way that does justice[22] to it, that is, a way which is universal enough to escape from the limitations of one particular perspective, and to open the door to a symbolic interpretation of whatever imagery may be used, then the Darwinist hypothesis is in danger, to say the least, of losing its hold. At the same time, in the light of the science of symbols, a new significance is seen in many features of sacred texts which are often dismissed as childish by the so-called higher criticism. The whole doctrine of the degrees of existence is implicit in what is said on the

[22] It has to be admitted that the religious fundamentalists, with their altogether literal interpretation of sacred texts have done much to undermine the traditional outlook in the eyes of many of those who are potentially intelligent but spiritually uninformed. Few things do more to further the acceptance of evolutionism than the fundamentalist assertion that the world was created in 4004 BC.

first page of the Old Testament about 'the dividing of the waters',[23] which is itself in fact the main division in the hierarchy of created things, the separation of the domain of the soul and the body from the domain of the Spirit.[24] Or let us take another example, the creation of man 'on the sixth day', which is highly significant, in the literal sense of the adverb here used. According to the symbolism of numbers, four denotes the terrestrial state, whence the quaternaries characteristic of it such as elements, seasons and points of the compass. Five denotes man's place at the centre of this state, his quintessentiality, whereas six, being 5 + 1, completes the full status of man by adding the transcendent dimension in virtue of which he is mediator[25] between Heaven and earth.

'The human form marks not only the summit of earthly creatures, but also—and for that very reason—the exit from their condition, or from the *samsara* as the Buddhists would say. To see man is to see not only the image of God but also a door open towards Bodhi, liberating Illumination; or let us say towards a blessed establishment in the divine Nearness . . . The animal, which can manifest perfections but not the Absolute, is like a closed door, as it were enclosed in its own perfection; whereas man is like an open door that allows him to escape his limits, which are those of the world rather than his own . . . The splendour of the stag excludes that of the lion, the eagle cannot be a swan, nor the water-lily the rose . . . only man is the image-synthesis of the Creator, by his possession of the intellect—thus also of reason and language—and by his manifestation of it through his very form.'[26]

For the evolutionist the whole issue is obscured by the absence from his perspective of any notion of normality. For him the

[23] For a parallel in Hinduism see René Guénon, *Man and his Becoming according to the Vedanta*, chapter v (closing paragraphs).

[24] That is, in its created aspect, for the Spirit has also and above all a Divine Aspect.

[25] It may be noted in this connection that in Arabic the letter *wāw* and in Hebrew the letter *vāv* both have the numerical value of six, and each constitutes, in its respective language, the linguistic mediator namely the word 'and'.

[26] Frithjof Schuon, *From the Divine to the Human*, p. 87.

human norm, which in its corporeal aspect is the theme of this last quotation, is a matter of fluctuating opinion. His beliefs oblige him, despite himself, to maintain that what might have seemed a norm for one age will be rejected by subsequent ages as 'primitive'. We say 'despite himself' because notwithstanding the widespread degeneration of the human race that shows itself above all in faces, almost everyone alive today has seen at least one or two examples of human beauty which bear the imprint of the Absolute and which, as his instinct must tell him, are therefore un-outdatable norms.

A book that is particularly relevant to our present context is *From the Divine to the Human*, from which we have just quoted. Its title proclaims in advance its timeliness for a world which, during the last hundred years or more, has been largely dominated by a supposition that might be expressed: 'from the subhuman to the human'. Schuon draws our attention to the significance of certain basic characteristics which all men have in common and which, if duly weighed, make it impossible to believe in the primacy of matter. There is not one of us who is not aware of powers within which are at an incomparably higher level than anything outward and visible. They could be summed up as our subjectivity and our objectivity, our subjective consciousness of being 'I', which is inextricably bound up with the mystery of life, and our objective intelligence, which is capable of grasping truths that infinitely transcend our empirical experience.

An argument of great importance which has been neglected by the official representatives of religion is that 'the ideas of the "Great Spirit" and the primacy of the Invisible are natural to man, a fact which does not need to be demonstrated', and that, 'what is natural to human consciousness proves *ipso facto* its essential truth inasmuch as the intelligence exists for no other reason than to be adequate to reality.' Analogously we could say that the existence of the ear proves the existence of sound; or as Schuon remarks: 'We have heard it said that the wings of birds prove the existence of air, and that in the same way the religious phenomenon, common *a priori* to all peoples, proves the existence of its content, namely God and the after-life: which is to the point if one takes the trouble to examine the argument in depth'.[27] The symbolism here is in itself illuminating, for religion gives man 'wings' and the air in question is the domain of the Transcendent for which those wings are made and the reality of which they 'prove'. It is true that such proofs are 'inaccessible to certain minds'; but Schuon gives also arguments of common sense, such as might convince some of those who are not—or not yet—open to demonstrations on a higher plane.

'Those who uphold the evolutionist argument of an intellectual progress like to explain religious and metaphysical ideas by inferior psychological factors, such as fear of the unknown, childish hope of perpetual happiness, attachment to an imagery that has become dear, escape into dreams, and the desire to oppress others at small expense *et cetera*; how can one fail to see that such suspicions, presented shamelessly as demonstrated facts, comprise psychological inconsequences and impossibilities which cannot escape any impartial observer? If humanity was stupid for thousands of years, one cannot explain how it could have ceased being so, especially since this is supposed to have happened in a relatively very short space of time; and one can explain it still less when one observes with what intelligence and heroism it was stupid for so long and with what philosophic shortsightedness and moral decadence it has finally become "lucid" and "adult"'.[28]

On a considerably lower plane, but still in the context of much needed arguments neglected by religious authorities, let us revert briefly to the scientific refutations of evolution, more of which are now available[29] than the two books already mentioned. Such

27 *From the Divine to the Human*, p.6.

28 Ibid. p.12.

29 For example, *Cosmos and Transcendence* (Breaking through the Barrier of Scientific Belief) by Wolfgang Smith; *Evolution: A Theory in Crisis*, by Michael Denton; and *Adam and Evolution* by Michael Pitman.

writings would be less necessary if evolutionist scientists were not so 'religiously' bent on converting men to the belief that the rise of the human from the subhuman is a proven fact. But things being as they are, it might have been expected that the various Christian Churches, and in particular the Roman Catholic Church, would not fail to take advantage of these refutations as powerful dispellers of an illusion which has drawn so many souls away from religion. No doubt under Pope Pius XII, the church would have made full use of such publications. But since his death, the Vatican has become interested above all in adapting Christianity to modern ideas and in showing that it is no longer 'behind the times'. It is not to be imagined that the man who made the following pronouncement could possibly be interested in a refutation of evolutionism; the speaker here is Paul VI; the occasion, the landing of the astronauts on the moon in 1971: 'Honour to Man, honour to thought, honour to science, honour to technique, honour to work, honour to the boldness of man, honour to the synthesis of scientific and organising ability of man who, unlike other animals, knows how to give his spirit and his manual dexterity these instruments of conquest. Honour to man king of the earth, and today Prince[30] of heaven'.[31] Later in the same year, he said: 'We moderns, men of our own day, wish everything to be new. Our old people, the Traditionalists, the Conservatives, measured the value of things according to their enduring quality. We instead, are actualists, we want everything to be new all the time, to be expressed in a continually improvised and dynamically unusual form.'[32]

He had already defined the 'Post-conciliar Church' by saying that it 'seeks to adapt itself to the languages, to the customs and

[30] It was the speaker of this 'litany' who eliminated, amongst other things, the prayer to St Michael, Prince of the Heavenly Hosts, at the end of the Mass. See also Verax, 'A Question Concerning the Second Vatican Council', published in *Studies in Comparative Religion*, and reproduced here with the author's permission, as Appendix C.

[31] Doc. Cath., No. 1580. See Rama Coomaraswamy, *The Destruction of the Christian Tradition*, p.95.

[32] Ibid. p.92.

to the inclinations of the men of our times, men completely engrossed in the rapidity of material evolution'. He also said: 'From the start the Council has propagated a wave of serenity and optimism, a Christianity that is exciting and positive, loving life, mankind and earthly values', and he added that the Council had 'an intention of making Christianity acceptable and lovable, indulgent and open, free from mediaeval rigorism and from the pessimistic understanding of man and his customs'.[33]

As to the present holder of the papal office, although, ironically enough, he is often referred to as a 'conservative', this does not apply to the essentials of worship, namely the Sacraments and the Liturgy. He is moreover, like Montini, an avowed admirer of Teilhard de Chardin, with an unbounded enthusiasm for modern man as such; and his choice of the name John-Paul was incontestably a pledge to maintain the innovations of his predecessors. In a word, until the death of Pope Pius XII, there was still one powerful organization in the West which implacably condemned the pseudo-religion of the modem world. But now that sole voice of condemnation has joined itself to the voices of complicity; and this cannot be without significance in relation to the question with which the chapter opened.

[33] *Doc. Cath.*, No. 1538.

4

The Political Extreme

THE ANALYSIS of a majority outlook which was the theme of the last chapter calls for something analogous in the domain of politics. It is often said that nations have the governments they deserve; and although many cases spring to mind of nations which might seem to merit better governments than they actually have, it is none the less true that unless there be interference from outside, a prevailing outlook is liable to bring down upon itself that form of rule which most nearly corresponds to it.

Apart from a few relatively small exceptions, the present day has little more than two possibilities of government to offer; and that limitation, considering what those possibilities are, is yet another significant sign of the times. To see it as such, we need only step for a moment outside the modern world in order to take a look at politics from a traditional standpoint, and one way of doing this will be to consider the whole question in the light of Plato's theory of government.

When Plato wrote his *Politeia* which might be translated 'State' or 'Polity', but which is most often, misleadingly, referred to as his 'Republic', he was answering a question which has been prominent in the minds of many thinking men and women of the Western world ever since the end of the Middle Ages: 'What is the ideal form of government?' If this question was not asked at other periods and in other regions, it was simply because, for the people concerned, it was not a question, the answer being too well known. Plato was a sage, but not a heavenly inspired and God-sent legislator, and he could therefore do no more than define his ideal state in theory. None the less, although his concept may seem highly questionable in some of its details, it corresponds in its essentials to every solution of Providence known to history inasmuch as it is no less than government according to transcendent principles which are summed up in the Absolute Good (*to Agathón*).[1] It is this essential aspect of Plato's state which concerns us here, and not its details.

But his epilogue is also directly related to our theme; for having made his definition, he remarks that even if his theory could be realized, even if such a state as he envisages could be actually established, it would be bound to lose its perfection and decline. 'Although a state so constituted will not easily be shaken, yet since all that is brought into existence is doomed to decay, even such a constitution as this will not endure forever but must needs come to dissolution.'[2] He then traces the different stages of decline, and in doing so he is foretelling, in general terms, much of what has happened since his day in various parts of the world. Aristocracy (rule by the best) is what Plato calls his ideal; then would follow timocracy, then oligarchy, then democracy, then tyranny. To convey Plato's conception in modern parlance, and keeping the term democracy, we could say theocracy for aristocracy and dictatorship or demagogy for tyranny. It is less easy to find a satisfactory term for the second and third forms of government, though it is clear that they can be taken together because they are structurally the same and because it is impossible to say exactly where one ends and the other begins. Moreover both are oligarchies—'rule by the few', that is, in most cases, a king and his peers, or a king and his favourites. Timocracy could be defined in Hindu terms as rule by Kshatriyas,[3] who have partly thrown off the authority of the Brahmins but who remain more or less true

[1] Plato, *Politeia*, VI, 508. [2] Ibid. VIII, 546. [3] The princely caste.

to their own nature; this becomes plutocracy—an alternative name which Plato gives for oligarchy, his third form of government—when for want of the upward pull of the caste above them, the nature of the Kshatriya rulers sinks downwards in the direction of the Vaisyas.[4] For want of a better term we could put these two governments jointly under the heading of traditional or principled autocracy, in virtue of the structural continuity which they have with the highest form of government, and because the principles are still recognized, however much they may come to be violated in fact.

It may be objected that the term 'traditional autocracy' or 'principled autocracy' is ambiguous, to which the obvious answer would be that the thing itself is not without ambiguity. In any case, it goes without saying that the words 'traditional' and 'principled' must be taken in a relative sense, since it is not traditional for the temporal power to be altogether autocratic, that is, independent of the spiritual authority. The form of government in question, being itself a breakaway from theocracy, is clearly less principled than the highest form of government. It none the less belongs to 'the old order of things' and is definitely on the side of tradition, though it is liable to end by bringing tradition into disrepute. Moreover autocracy is in itself dangerous owing to the highly explosive and volatile nature of human individuality in which it is vested; and there is always the risk that without any structural change a principled autocracy may become a *de facto* unprincipled dictatorship. To take one example, this could be said to have happened towards the end of the reign of Henry VIII, who had previously been principled enough to earn the title 'Defender of the Faith'.

Such exceptions apart, the next stage on the path of decline after principled autocracy is democracy in which, according to Plato, the dominant notions are liberty and equality. In this respect his concept coincides with the modern one. Democracy is also, in his

[4] The merchant caste.

opinion, the harbinger of demagogy or dictatorship; and although no twentieth-century democrat likes to think of it in this way, recent history has not proved that Plato is wrong, to say the least. Since degeneration tends to follow an undulating course, there are likely to be partial redresses here and there and from time to time which might seem, quite wrongly, to give the lie to Plato who is merely stating general tendencies and would have been the first to admit that degeneration is not a straight downward slope. It is always possible, for example, that when a democracy ends in chaos, as it seems fated often to do, a principled autocrat may come to the rescue instead of the much to be dreaded unprincipled demagogue. Such was the case in recent Spanish history when Franco re-established a principled autocracy, that is, a Christian kingdom, with himself as regent, thus saving his country from a communist dictatorship. The democracy which preceded this restoration was very short-lived; and sometimes, owing to the lack of resistance inherent in this form of government, a democracy may be superseded at the moment of birth.

The French Revolution was democratic in its original intention—witness the slogan *Liberté, Egalité, Fraternité* (the meaningless third term being thrown in as a sop to human sentiment)—but in fact the fall was too precipitous to stop at democracy, so that the change from principled autocracy to unprincipled demagogy was almost direct. The time was not yet ripe however for this lowest form of government to last, and it was superseded by Napoleon's relatively principled autocracy. But 125 years later, what might be called cosmic or cyclic pressures had changed, and Russia had no Napoleon to save her from almost 80 years of what is probably the lowest ebb to which government can sink. It is not however the lowest form of government which inaugurates the rejection of principles. To pave the way for unprincipled dictatorship, the principles have first of all to be rejected by democracy[5] in the name

[5] Already in democracy, according to Plato, the principles are 'trampled under foot'. (VIII, 558).

of 'liberty'. For Plato true liberty is no less than the escape from the 'cave' of this world and its limitations. The way of escape which he calls 'the rugged and steep ascent' is 'the narrow gate' of the Gospels, 'and few are they that find it'. These few are the philosophers who would be the rulers of Plato's aristocracy, and whose task it is to see that their subjects are directed towards the transcendent principles and therefore towards the narrow gate beyond which the principles lie. To face in this direction necessarily means the curtailing of a lower liberty—a discipline which is tolerated so long as the philosophers are there to remind their subjects that it is for the sake of a higher liberty.

Every theocracy is grounded on the truth that this life is no more than a bridge to the next, and on the rule 'Seek ye first the Kingdom of God and his righteousness, and all these things (the necessities of this world) shall be added unto you.' (Matthew, VII, 33)—a truth and a rule which are formulated in various ways from religion to religion, and which can never be absent. But degeneration, which nothing in this world can escape, means moving away from the principles. The movement does not at first necessitate a change of orientation: communities slip slowly backwards down 'the steep ascent' while still looking up towards the narrow gate which marks its summit. But gradually the justification of the discomfort of facing in this direction is lost sight of, until there comes a point when the majority of people decide to turn their backs on the principles. This means an immediate and powerful sensation of liberty—for 'wide is the gate and broad is the way'—but it is liberty on a lower plane. As Frithjof Schuon writes: 'In all cases of this kind, heaven—or a heaven—is shut off from above us without our noticing the fact and we discover in compensation an earth long unappreciated, or so it seems to us, a homeland which opens its arms to welcome its children and wants to make us forget all lost Paradises.'[6] Very relevant also is what he says in particular of the Renaissance which was one of the great milestones of decline in

[6] *Light on the Ancient Worlds*, p.29.

Western Europe: 'Man as such had become to all intents and purposes good, and the earth too had become good and looked immensely rich and unexplored; instead of living only "by halves" one could at last live fully, be fully man and fully on earth; one was no longer a kind of half-angel, fallen and exiled; one had become a whole being, but by the downward path.'[7]

The turning of one's back on the principles does not yet mean that they are totally disregarded. That is only the case when a later stage is reached, which corresponds to the establishment of the democratic state. With regard to this and to the even less principled system that it often leads to, our own times are particularly instructive. We are living in the very age of democracy and dictatorship, since these are the inevitable outcome of moving away from the principles, and it is at the end of the temporal cycle that man is furthest from his transcendent origins. Let us therefore consider, in the 'light' of our times, a significant feature of each of these two lowest forms of government. As regards democracy it may be noted that the so-called 'free world' is not so free as to have escaped from compulsory education. 'Equality' has here been given precedence over 'liberty'. Everyone must be given 'an equal chance' for the start of life. This means that everyone must be indoctrinated with relativism. Pupils are taught that our ancestors believed in principles which they regarded as absolute, but that in our day the principles are questioned by most 'thinking people'. There is practically never any suggestion that certain kinds of knowledge are more important than others. To establish a hierarchy would be to violate the very notion of equality and to paralyse 'freedom of thought'. It is impressed on all that every man, woman, boy and girl have a right to their own opinions, unless they can be proved wrong logically or scientifically. Otherwise unusual opinions may be applauded for their originality. Everyone is encouraged to think for himself or herself; but the manner of

[7] Ibid. pp. 29–30.

teaching ensures, as we have already seen, that the ground is steeply sloped in favour of agnosticism, progressism and evolutionism.

Under the lowest form of government a compulsory uniform 'official' education teaches categorically that religion was a purely human invention for the purpose of intimidating and oppressing the mass of the people, and that the principles simply do not exist. In a word, our times have taught us that the difference between democracy and dictatorship is as the difference between allowing evil (and therefore also good) and enforcing evil.[8]

The sudden disintegration of the most powerful and most extensive of the dictatorships clearly cannot be thought of as an undoing of the harm that it had already done. For four generations the inhabitants of the vast tract of territory which made up the Soviet Union had been forcibly indoctrinated with atheism, the worst of all evils, together with all the lesser lies that uphold it; and for two generations the rest of what lay behind 'the iron curtain' had been held in the same grip of perversion. That it should not have succeeded in every individual case was inevitable, but with the majority it prevailed; and in certain respects the evil it has done cannot fail to be augmented by closer contact with those 'free world' evils against which the 'curtain' had served as a protection.

On the other hand we must rejoice in the restoration of power to the spiritual authority to exercise fully their power and in the disappearance of communist education, which means the replacement of that greater evil by the lesser evil of Western education. This makes for considerably more freedom to take advantage of the positive aspects of the eleventh hour, which are the main theme of the next chapter.

In more general terms, since this hour is a period of transition, it

[8] Not that Plato was unaware of this, since according to him the demagogue or tyrant, inasmuch as he 'purges' the state of all its best elements, leaving only the worst, is the exact opposite of the healer. When speaking of the healer he no doubt has in mind the philosopher-kings who would rule his aristocracy.

was no doubt necessary that the solidified rigid chaos of communism should give way to the more fluid chaos of the West. It must not, however be forgotten that the menacing presence of the Soviet and its satellites engendered, in the 'free world', a salutary sense of danger which brought about, in some democracies, a marked stiffening in favour of conservation. An increasing number of individuals were won over to being defenders of principles and upholders of tradition. Also, as regards political structure, it would no doubt be true to say that the more a democracy is still penetrated with the residues of principled autocracy, the more resistant it is likely to be against unprincipled tyranny; and it is to be feared that those residues may now be endangered by a false sense of security.

If our times are instructive at the lowest level, no times are less instructive as regards the nature of theocracy. The most recent of Providence's solutions to the problem of government was realized some 1400 years ago with the founding of the first Islamic state in Medina. At its outset it was miraculously successful. The initial perfection was short-lived, although thanks to detailed records it remains to this day as an ideal, an example and a criterion. Every effort has been made to keep it clear in the minds of men, and Islam has in a sense lived on it throughout the centuries. Embodying as it does the practices and recommendations of the God-sent Messenger, this ideal constitutes the second spiritual authority of the religion, the first being the Revelation itself. The third authority, incomparably less than the other two, with no power to make any fundamental changes whatsoever, lies in a certain consensus of reliable opinion among Muslims themselves. But if the spiritual authority among men is limited in Islam, it is by compensation exceedingly widespread. It is sometimes affirmed that every man is a priest; at any rate, there is no laity, and it cannot be denied that a sharp and implacable awareness of what God has ordained and what the Prophet has recommended is to be found in a multitude of individuals throughout the Islamic world. After the first four Caliphs, who continue to be revered as Saints, the highest posts have been held by relatively few good men. The saying 'Power and Paradise go not together' soon came to be accepted almost as a truism. But the dearth of good rulers was unable to shake the theocracy in its immutable adamantine structure. Thanks to this, and to the widespread spiritual alertness among believers, the world of Islam was able to take other severe tests in its stride. A pagan conqueror like Hulagu, grandson of Ghengis Khan, could sweep over Persia, Iraq and Syria, raze Baghdad, the seat of the caliphate, to the ground, put most of its men to the sword, including the Caliph and all his family. But what then? The lands in question—it was 1258 AD—were only governable in one way. By the end of the century the Mongol dynasty had become the champions of Islam and the lavish patrons of its arts. Needless to say, Islam is not the only true religion to have absorbed its pagan conquerors. Other analogous examples are to be found elsewhere, but those we have just mentioned are particularly striking, and they are significant also, as we shall see, in view of their place in the temporal cycle.

Modernists argue that in such cases the conquered civilization was only able to prevail owing to the limitations of the conquerors, who had nothing positive to offer. What they have in mind is obvious, but it is grounded on more than one error, including the total failure to see the modern so-called 'civilization' from any standpoint but its own, which they themselves incarnate. Seen in a wider perspective, the thing in question appears as nothing other than an inevitable aspect of extreme old age—the old age of the world. It cannot rightly be called a civilization if we are to go on speaking of the Hindu, Buddhist, Christian and Islamic civilizations, to take only four examples, which are the most important. The purpose of all these—and of their analogues—was to preserve such of man's primordial heritage as had been partially restored by the Revelations on which their respective religions are based, and to retard the inevitable process of degeneration. Of all that they stood for, the modern 'civilization' is the direct antithesis, for it is nothing other than an organized system of subversion and degeneration. Instead of trying to resist the natural downward tendencies of man, the movement away from the principles, from the higher to the lower, from the inward to the outward, it welcomes and encourages them in the name of progress and evolution.

The impact of the West on the traditional civilizations has been to accelerate greatly a process of degeneration which was already taking place, and to give them, as it were, a sideways push to ensure that they went downhill by a steeper and somewhat different course from the one they were following. The world of Islam has had more than 700 years in which to degenerate since the sack of Baghdad, and its people are correspondingly less resistant. But despite the new direction and the new speed that its degeneration has taken, the Islamic civilization is still relatively within reach.

A Christian civilization in the full sense of the term is, on the contrary, out of reach. Plato stresses the extreme importance of externals in the ideal state, namely that people should be surrounded from their earliest years by the right objects; and it has been a marked characteristic of every theocratic civilization known to history that its outward features, including garments, were determined and controlled according to the principles of sacred art. Already a betrayal in this respect was the Church's acceptance of the Renaissance, which has remained as an almost insurmountable barrier between Western Europe and Christendom in the fullest sense of this term.

In any case, the Western world is no longer theocratically governable. No community in the West is sufficiently open to transcendent truths for there to be so much as a necessary minimum of individuals capable of discerning the difference between a legally enforced restraint based on those truths and a tyranny based on arbitrary human opinion. From the point of view of modern democratic education, both the restraints in question are tyrannies. How few are capable of distinguishing, for example, between a principled autocracy like that of recent Spain, and dictatorships like those of Hitler, Stalin, and Mao; and if a principled autocracy is labelled tyranny, how much less tolerance would there be for theocracy, which would necessarily interfere with men's lives in far more intimate details. How little understood was the recent tragedy of traditional Tibet! The brutality of its overthrow was abhorred, and so was the tyrannical nature of the act; but few Western tears were shed for what was lost.[9] The fact, however, that such a theocracy could have existed so recently suggests that the situation in the East is still very different from that in the West, despite the spell that is cast upon Orientals by modern science and modern inventions, and despite the impact of Western education. In most of the East the principles are still recognized; and if something can be shown to be in obedience to them, there is a chance that it may be tolerated.

These remarks should not be allowed to engender any sanguine illusions about the state of the world. But it may well be asked how far anything in the nature of a political restoration might now be possible, nor could any assessment of the present day be complete without giving that question some sort of answer. Let us therefore consider once again, by way of example, that particular religious community which was founded by the most recent of the God-sent messengers and which has thus had less time than others to degenerate. Firstly, it must be remembered that a providential intervention which establishes a new religion may be said to have, in virtue of the immensity of its scope, a double aspect. There are elements which wholly or partly escape from time, and there are elements which are subject to time. As we have already seen in

[9] The modern civilization had been expressly excluded from Tibet. Not even a bicycle was allowed across the frontier. What tyranny! And how Socrates would have applauded it!

another connection,[10] the spirituality which is established with the new religion is itself above time, and therefore does not have to grow or develop, but begins at its highest point. This point corresponds in Islam to the presence of Muhammad and his Companions, and in Christianity to the presence of Christ and his Apostles. From such a summit there can only be a decline; but the Prophet of Islam promised 'God will send to this community, at the head of every hundred years, one who will renew for it its religion'; and there have been analogous graces for all other religions. These renewals are like rhythmic reverberations, echoes of the initial great renewal which brought into existence the religion itself. As such they also may be said to escape in a sense from the domination of time. On the other hand, the outer aspects of a theocracy are subject to time, and therefore to the phases of gradual waxing and waning. The act of Divine Revelation, or the mission of a Divine Messenger, must therefore be said to include the sowing of the seeds of a theocratic civilization which will take a certain time to grow to fullness, and which will then inevitably decay. Its fullness means the realization of outward conditions which are especially favourable to spirituality,[11] and which will therefore serve to increase the impact of such of the 'renewals' as take place during this period which they, in their turn, will help to prolong. Once the fullness has been reached, the great function of the spiritual authority and the temporal power is to protect it against change. The excellence of the first century of Islam lay above all in the excellence of its men and women. It had also an outward perfection by reason of its closeness to virgin nature. Unlike Christianity, it was still, at its birth, nomadic or semi-nomadic. The initial Islamic community in Mecca and Medina at the time of the Prophet had, in its outward aspects, the perfection of primordial simplicity. But wherever that simplicity was abandoned, it became immediately clear that an Islamic civili-

[10] See p.21.

[11] See Frithjof Schuon, *Treasures of Buddhism*, pp. 136–137.

zation in the ordinary sense had not yet had time to grow.[12] The seventh century of Islam might perhaps be said to mark the plenitude in question, though clearly one would not want to insist too much on this. Analogously, in speaking of human life, one may prefer not to limit the concept of maturity to one age only. However that may be, the seventh century of Islam[13]—and let us include with it also the eighth—could no doubt be said to correspond to the latest and therefore most accessible point of non-degeneration for the Islamic world. Since then there has been a gradual decline, retarded on the one hand by the 'renewers' who have not ceased to come—although there is less and less that they can achieve except in the domain of esoterism, that is, for a minority—and on the other hand by human efforts of spiritual conservation which the West has been pleased to call 'stagnation'. But it is precisely thanks to this 'stagnation' that the Islamic civilization, unlike the Christian one, could still be pieced together, structurally speaking. It would also probably be true to say that the mass of the people is still theocratically governable in most Islamic countries. But the active and dominant few are not. The call for one's country to become 'a modern nation with an internationally acceptable government' is altogether typical of the average 'enlightened' Near and Middle Eastern politician, industrialist, teacher, and their like. Nor in any case could there be an effective return to the Islamic civilization in the true sense so long as the modern civilization still exists, since the two are incompatible. It would be altogether inadequate simply to change the legal system from profane law to Islamic law, which many seem to think is all that need be done. A whole network of far-reaching changes would be necessary, if the civilization were to be spiritually operative.[14]

[12] To see this, one has only to look, for example, at the remains of the Umayyad palaces in Jericho.

[13] That is, the thirteenth century AD.

[14] There would moreover be need for an extreme subtlety of discrimination to decide exactly what restorations were to be effected and what were to be avoided. Certain

Meantime a minority of intellectuals might re-establish a traditional framework for themselves and have the spiritual benefits it offers, while keeping the modern world at bay by all sorts of compromises which only they would know how to make. But whole nations could become traditionally civilized only if and when the modern 'civilization' is taken from them by force.

When in the past a traditional civilization collapsed, it was inevitably replaced, sooner or later, by another traditional civilization. There was no modern civilization lying in ambush and waiting to take over. The present state of affairs has no parallel in the history of the world; and since it is the external crystallization of the progressist and evolutionist outlook of twentieth-century man, it has been mentioned here as a sign parallel to that more inward sign, and as a parallel answer to the question asked at the outset of the preceding chapter.

---

superficial aspects of the Islamic civilization are in direct contradiction with Islam's claim to be the primordial religion; and it is much to be doubted whether the restoration of such aspects would be cyclically possible.

5

The Spirit of the Times

ACCORDING TO world-wide tradition, the 'life' of the macrocosm consists of thousands of years of spiritual prosperity leading gradually down, from Golden Age to Silver Age to Bronze Age, until it reaches a relatively short final period[1] in which the prosperity is increasingly marred by its opposite. This period, the Iron Age or, as the Hindus term it, the Dark Age, is the late autumn and the winter of the cycle, and it roughly coincides with what is called 'historic' as opposed to 'prehistoric'. All old age, both macrocosmic and microcosmic, has its ills. But normal old age has also its wisdom; and half hidden behind the negative signs which we see on all sides, our day has also something positive to offer which is characteristic of no previous era and which is, as such, yet another sign of the times.

Needless to say, this is not a claim that old age alone is endowed with wisdom, or that, analogously, our times excel in that respect—far from it. Humanity is the heart of the macrocosm and the four ages of the cycle are what they are according to the state of mankind. The pre-excellence of the Golden Age derives from the

[1] According to Hinduism, which has the oldest and most explicit doctrine of the cycles, the first age is the longest and the fourth is the shortest. The Genesis commentaries and the Jewish apocryphal books make it clear that there is no mutual contradiction between the perspective of the monotheistic religions and the pre-biblical doctrine of four ages (see *Ancient Beliefs and Modern Superstitions*, pp. 20–22).

spirituality—which implies wisdom—of mankind in general. This whole was subsequently reduced to being no more than a majority which was then reduced to a minority, ultimately a small one. It can none the less be said that there is a mode of wisdom which belongs to old age in particular, and which is even susceptible of being assimilated, to a certain degree, by those who were not wise in youth and middle age. The old age of the cycle is bound to be a congenial setting for it; and the following passage gives us a hint of a collective or macrocosmic wisdom which belongs to our times precisely by reason of their lateness.

'The usual religious arguments, through not probing sufficiently to the depth of things and moreover not having previously had any need to do so, are psychologically somewhat outworn and fail to satisfy certain requirements of causality. If human societies degenerate on the one hand with the passage of time, they accumulate on the other hand experiences in virtue of old age, however intermingled with errors these may be. This paradox is something that any pastoral teaching intended to be effective should take into account, not by drawing new directives from the general error, but on the contrary by using arguments of a higher order, intellectual rather than sentimental.'[2]

In the phrase 'human societies' the plural reminds us that the modern world is not the only human world that has degenerated with the passage of time. Each of the four ages may be said to constitute in itself a lesser cycle, beginning with a 'youth' and ending with an 'eld'; and there are yet lesser cycles within them—for example, the civilization of ancient Egypt, or that of ancient Rome. In all these lesser cycles there must have been in some degree, towards the end, an accumulation of 'experience in virtue of old age'. The twentieth century, together with the decades which immediately follow it, would appear to constitute the final phase of that particular human society which may be said to have been established in Europe—with eventual prolongations—about

[2] Frithjof Schuon, *In the Face of the Absolute*, pp.89–90.

1500 years ago. It is also, in a parallel way, the final phase of many other societies—Hindu, American Indian, Jewish, Buddhist and Islamic—which have been partially merged into one with the Western world by the super-imposition of its way of life over their own traditional differences from it and from each other. But at the same time we are living at the very end of one of the four ages; and since it is the last of the four, its end will be the end of the great cycle of all four ages taken as a whole. In other words, we are now participating in the extreme old age of the macrocosm, which is to be followed by a new cycle of four ages.

It may be objected that in view of the immense length of the cycle the macrocosm could be said to have reached its old age long before the twentieth century. That is true, but the old age in question was overlaid by the youth of subsidiary cycles. Two thousand years ago, the incipient twilight of the great cycle receded before the dawn of Christianity, which was followed later by the dawn of Islam; and even as recently as 700 years ago there took place what has been called the 'second birth' of Christianity: it was the time of the building of the great cathedrals and the founding of many of the orders of mysticism. Christendom had been allowed a 'fresh flowering', precariously set though it was within the old age of the great cycle. It could not last: all too quickly and easily it was drawn into the main cosmic current of degeneration. The same applies to the already mentioned 'second birth' of Islam[3] which partly coincided in time with that of Christianity inasmuch as Christendom took considerably longer to develop than the civilization of Islam. It is true that the younger religion still retained something of its youth when its elder sister could no longer be called young in any sense. But today there is nothing to modify the greater cycle's old age which is, on the contrary, reinforced by the old age of all the lesser cycles which it contains. It can therefore be said, macrocosmically speaking, that all men alive today, whatever their years, are 'old'; and the question

[3] See p.51.

arises, for each individual, which aspect of old age, the positive or the negative, will he or she represent in the macrocosm, that is, in the human collectivity taken as a whole, and how active or passive will each be in this respect.

As regards what Schuon says about pastoral teaching that is no longer effective, the dogma that there is only one valid religion, namely 'ours', may serve as an example of an argument that is 'psychologically somewhat outworn'. Such teachings 'fail to satisfy certain requirements of causality' because they are now seen to defeat one of the main ends of religion which is to bestow a sense of the Glory of God. Modern man cannot help having a broader view of the world than his ancestors had, partly through the destruction of the protective walls of the different traditional civilizations—in itself a tragedy—and partly through the enormously increased facilities of travel and the corresponding increase of information which is poured into his mind through various channels. This broader view may enable him to be impressed by religions other than his own, and at the very least it compels him to see that their existence makes the world-wide spread of his own religion impossible. If they were false, what of the Glory of Him who allowed them to establish themselves, with their millennial roots, over so vast an area?

For those who are not prepared to sacrifice that Glory to human prejudices, it has become abundantly clear that none of the so-called 'world religions' can have been intended by Providence to establish itself over the whole globe. The question does not arise with those forms of worship like Hinduism and Judaism which are specifically for one people only. But Buddhism, Christianity and Islam, though each is virtually open to everybody, have also beyond doubt their particular sectors of humanity; and though the frontiers may be difficult to define, and though Islam, the most recently revealed of the three, is in the nature of things likely to continue gaining ground in many directions, it seems probable to say the least that the three sectors will remain largely the same until the end of the age. But if such an objective view of religion is widespread, this is not for the most part due to an increase of acuity in the intelligence, but rather to the fact that an 'old man' cannot help being 'experienced'. Otherwise expressed, it is due to a mainly passive participation in the positive aspects of the present age. For anyone who is intellectually active however, this universal outlook is a secondary accompanying asset—albeit none the less necessary—of what may be called 'the spirit of the times'.

To see what is meant by this, let us consider in more detail the characteristics of old age. To speak of the 'old age' of the macrocosm is not merely to speak in metaphor. According to a doctrine that is to be found, variously expressed, in all religions, there is a real analogical correspondence between macrocosm and microcosm, a correspondence which is implicit in these terms themselves, 'great world' and 'little world'. This universal doctrine enables us to grasp certain elusive aspects of the macrocosm through the corresponding aspects of the microcosm; and the ambiguous, dividedly dual nature of our times can be better understood if we consider in more detail the old age of the microcosm or, more precisely, of the normal microcosm, for he alone is the true counterpart of the macrocosm.

The word normal is used here in its strict sense, as the epithet of that which is a norm: only man as he was created, or one who has regained the primordial state, True Man as the Taoists call him, can be considered as a full microcosm, whose life corresponds to the 'life' of the macrocosm, that is, to the cycle of time which is now nearing its close; and by extension from True Man, that is, from the Saint, we might include in the human norm every truly spiritual man who has at least a virtual wholeness, even if it be not yet fully realized.

Like the macrocosm, the normal microcosm is subject in old age to the tension of two opposite tendencies, a contradiction which in the first part of life was relatively latent and from which, in the Earthly Paradise, man was altogether exempt. This contradiction is due to the imprisonment of an immortal soul in a mortal body, a soul which is moreover in communion with the Spirit. The body is an image of the soul, of which it is also a prolongation. In youth, generally speaking, the body appears as a purely positive symbol and there is perfect harmony between it and the soul. Analogous to this is the harmonious homogeneity of the earlier ages of the macrocosmic cycle. But gradually, in the microcosm, the body begins to show that it is merely a symbol, and that 'merely' becomes more and more aggravated with the passage of time. On the one hand, therefore, there is a gradual bodily deterioration which ends with death; on the other hand there is a mellowing of spirituality. The serene and objective wisdom which is the central characteristic of normal old age outweighs, by its transcendence, the many ills which are the inevitable result of increasing decrepitude,[4] and in a certain sense it may be said to thrive on them. The corresponding ills of the macrocosm likewise create a climate which is not unfavourable to wisdom on condition that they are seen as ills. Detachment is an essential feature of the sage, and this virtue, which in better times could only be acquired through great spiritual efforts, can be made more spontaneous by the sight of one's world in chaotic ruins.

There is yet another feature of normal old age, the most positive of all, which likewise has its macrocosmic equivalent, in virtue of which our times are unique. It is sometimes said of spiritual men and women at the end of their lives that they have 'one foot already in Paradise'. This is not meant to deny that death is a sudden break, a rupture of continuity. It cannot but be so, for it has to transform mortal old age into immortal youth. None the less, hagiography teaches us that the last days of sanctified souls can be remarkably luminous and transparent. Nor is it unusual that the imminence of death should bring with it special graces, such as visions, in foretaste of what is to come. The mellowing of

[4] By way of example we may consider on the one hand the blindness which befell both Isaac and Jacob in extreme old age, and on the other hand their inward illumination.

spirituality, which is the highest aspect of old age in itself, is thus crowned with an illumination which belongs more to youth than to age; and it is to this synthesis, or more precisely to its macrocosmic counterpart, that the title of our chapter refers; for analogously, in the macrocosm, the nearness of the new Golden Age cannot fail to make itself mysteriously felt before the end of the old cycle; and, as we shall see later, such an anticipation has been predicted in various parts of the globe. We have here, in this junction of ending with beginning, yet another reason, perhaps the most powerful of all, why 'the last shall be first'.[5]

The decrepitude of the macrocosm in its old age is the theme of the two preceding chapters of this book; and to those ailments already mentioned we may add the many pseudo-esoterisms and heresies with which the modern world is rife, and which make it easier to go astray than ever before. Despite these, thanks to what is most positive in this day of conflicting opposites, the highest and deepest truths have become correspondingly more accessible, as if forced to unveil themselves by cyclic necessity, the macrocosm's need to fulfil its aspect of terminal wisdom. This same need—for to speak of wisdom is to speak of esoterism—was bound to cause an inward movement away from error and towards these truths. That it has in fact done so is shown, apart from more direct but less accessible signs, by the greatly increased publication of relevant books, for a minority no doubt but none the less on a scale to which esoterism has long been unaccustomed. The complex nature of the spirit of the times can explain facts which could otherwise be difficult to account for. In this meeting of estuary and source, finality derives from primordiality a certain aspect of abruptness, an initiative which is not typical of old age itself. Needless to say, the movement in question could not be lacking in the necessary traditional continuity; but neither could it be a smooth transition, an ordinary sequel from something that has gone before; and this explains also the

[5] See p.11.

widespread lack of preparation for it. Amongst those who in themselves are truly qualified for an esoteric path, it is inevitable that not a few should stand in need of a certain initial enlightenment by reason of their upbringing and education in the modern world.

This applies in yet greater measure to others, less qualified and more numerous, who in an earlier age would probably have remained in exoterism and who appear to owe their eventual qualification for esoterism partly to the fact of their birth in the present age. The following quotation will help to explain this paradox: 'Exoterism is a precarious thing by reason of its limits or its exclusions; there comes a moment in history when all kinds of experiences oblige it to modify its claims to exclusiveness, and it is then driven to a choice: escape from these limitations by the upward path, in esoterism, or by the downward path, in a worldly and suicidal liberalism. As one might have expected, the civilizationist exoterism of the West has chosen the downward path, while combining this incidentally with a few esoteric notions which in such conditions remain inoperative.'[6]

This lower choice, officially ratified by Vatican II for the Catholic Church and already characteristic of the other Churches of Western Europe, does not prevent individuals from choosing the upward path, that of esoterism. Some of those who would not have been qualified in the past are now given access to it in virtue of a truly positive attitude, severely put to the test by the present spiritual crisis, and amply verified by the choice of the higher rather than the lower. On the one hand, the foundering of certain

[6] Frithjof Schuon, *Esoterism as Principle and as Way*, pp.19–20. By way of example, the acceptance of religions other than one's own is esoterically operative if it be based on intellectual discernment between the true and the false, that is, if it be recognition of orthodoxy to the exclusion of everything else. But acceptance of other religions on the basis of the widely predominant sentimental pseudo-charity of our day is not merely inoperative in any positive sense but it is exceedingly harmful, for where discernment is not the guiding factor the door to error is inevitably opened, and the true religions are dishonoured by being placed on a level with heretical sects.

exoteric vessels is bound in the nature of things to enlarge the responsibilities of esoterism, which cannot refuse to take on board those in the sea about it who ask for a lifeline to be thrown to them and who have no means of salvation else. On the other hand, obtusenesses which in the past would have proved to be disqualifications can be modified or even partially dissolved by the virtues inherent in 'old age'. Whatever the circumstances may be, a suppliant hand held out from the modern chaos in the direction of right guidance is an indication that its owner cannot be relegated to the spiritually passive majority.

In connection with the widespread need for initial enlightenment, it must be remembered that esoterism presupposes the sense of the Absolute. More precisely, since there is no soul which is not virtually imbued with this sense, esoterism presupposes that it be actual and operative, at least to a certain degree. On that basis it can be further actualized by indirect contact with the Absolute, that is, with Its 'overflows', if one may use such a term, into the various domains of this world. One such 'overflow' is the esoteric doctrine itself, and this is indispensable; but its effect upon the soul may be reinforced by other earthly manifestations of the Absolute. The argument of beauty, for example, may be a powerful ally to the arguments of truth.

In the theocratic civilizations, the spiritual authority and the temporal power saw to it that the beauty of nature was not unduly desecrated by man, and that parallel to nature there were objects of sacred art that conformed to a style which had come as a gift from Heaven, and which was never a merely human invention. In the rigorous sense of the term, which is all we are considering here, sacred art is as a crystallization of sanctity, a spiritual presence which has power to purify and to enlighten and which, unlike ascetic practices of a similar power, makes no demands of man which run counter to his natural bent.

'It[7] sets up, against the sermon which insists on what must be

[7] Sacred art, and in particular the architecture of mediaeval Christendom.

done by one who would become holy, a vision of the cosmos which is holy through its beauty; it makes men participate naturally and almost involuntarily in the world of holiness.'[8]

Today, despite the desecrations, nature still remains an inexhaustible treasury of reminders to man of his true heritage, reminders which may become operative in the light of the doctrine; and parallel to virgin nature, even if the Christian civilization may have gone without possibility of recall, many of its landmarks still remain. Some of these, the cathedrals for example, are monuments of overwhelming beauty which bear witness to the spiritual exaltation of the age which produced them. In addition to their power as sacred art, they are eloquent exponents—and never more so than when seen from today's abyss—of spirituality's universal rule; 'Seek ye first the Kingdom of Heaven and all the rest shall be given unto you', and its parallel 'Unto him that hath shall be given'. At the same time, their presence is yet another demonstration of the truth that 'from him that hath not shall be taken away even that which he hath'. As material objects, they proclaim the spiritual man's mastery over matter, whereas the inability of the modern world to produce anything like them betrays the materialist's impotence precisely where he might have been expected to excel. He it is 'that hath not', having rejected the Transcendent; and 'that which he hath', namely matter, is taken away from him in the sense that he cannot really be said to possess it, having no qualitative dominion over it. We have only to approach a town like New York to have an alarming impression that matter has taken possession of man and quantitatively overwhelmed him. But standing in front of Durham, Lincoln or Chartres Cathedral we see that our mediaeval ancestors were able to dominate matter to the point of compelling it to excel itself and to become vibrant with the Spirit.

What has been said about Christian art applies also to the arts of

[8] Titus Burckhardt, *Sacred Art in East and West*, p.46. The message of this book is centrally typical of the wisdom of the age both in virtue of its universality and of its finality.

other sacred civilizations; and for the great loss of the experience of a traditional way of life, there can now be, for those capable of taking it, a certain compensation in the gain of access to the spiritual riches of traditions other than one's own. Religions in their outermost aspects have often been represented as different points on the circumference of a circle, the centre of which is the Divine Truth. Every such point is connected to the centre by a radius which stands for the esoterism of the religion in question. The more a radius approaches the centre, the nearer it is to the other radii, which illustrates the fact that the esoteric paths are increasingly close to each other, however far the respective exoterisms may seem to be; and sacred art, although it does not withhold its blessings from any sector of the community, is in itself a purely esoteric phenomenon, which means that it is central and therefore universal. Needless to say, there are degrees to be observed in this respect; but all that is best in sacred art virtually belongs to everyone who has 'eyes to see' or 'ears to hear', no matter what his faith or his race; and this virtuality can be actualized today as never before.

The nearer a work is to the centre the more universal it is, but also, at the same time, the more concentratedly it represents the world of its own particular provenance. What could be more universal than the Bharata Natyam temple dancing of India and the music that accompanies it, the landscape paintings of China and Japan, the Romanesque and Gothic cathedrals of Western Europe, and the mosques of Andalusia, Egypt, Persia and Turkestan, to mention only a few examples? And what, respectively, could give us a more concentrated sense of the unique spiritual fragrance of each of the four ways in question, Hinduism, Taoism, Christianity and Islam? To add a fifth, exactly the same may be said of the statuary of Buddhism, from Ajanta to Kyoto. Taken together, the summits of sacred art give us in little, that is, in an easily assimilated form, a faithful view of the immense variety of the great religions and their civilizations, a pageant which can be for some as a semi-transparent veil that both hides and reveals the Transcendent Source of these wonders.[9] This comprehensive view may be considered as an aspect of that wisdom which is the theme of our chapter; for although it is a potential feature of every sage, no matter when he lives, it withheld itself as an actuality from all other epochs, and offers itself now to him who seeks.'[10]

What has been said about the crystallization of holiness in art may be said to hold good for incarnations of holiness, the sainthoods which exemplify the primordial nature that is hidden in fallen man by second nature. Some men can be initially penetrated and won more easily by a personal perfection, a human summit, than by any other mode of excellence; and there can now be added, to the Saints of one religion's calendar, their glorious counterparts from every other religion. We are speaking here of an initial penetration, and of indirect contacts with holy men such as can be made through the reading of hagiographies. It goes without saying that at a later stage the living personal perfection of the Spiritual Master[11] will necessarily take precedence, while at the same time it will make these other examples of sainthood more accessible.

As to the doctrine, it is indispensable both in itself and to throw its light on other motivations. It is also needed today as a protection: if esoteric truths continued to be kept secret as in the past on account of their danger, this would not prevent the spread of pseudo-esoterism, a poison to which the best antidote is true esoterism whose dangers are thus outweighed by its powers to safeguard against its own counterfeits; and beyond these it is

[9] In the Islamic litany of the 99 Names of God, one of the names which this context recalls is *al-Badīʿ*, the Marvellously Original.

[10] The quantities of lavishly illustrated books now available, and their equivalents for the auditive arts, are yet another sign of the times inasmuch as they spring from what might be called the archival aspect of finality, a question we will return to later.

[11] It is a universal axiom that anyone who is truly qualified to follow an esoteric path will find, if he 'seeks' and, if he 'knocks', the Master he needs. For more ample considerations on this subject, see Appendix B.

needed for the refutation of more general errors. 'We live in an age of confusion and thirst in which the advantages of communication are greater than those of secrecy; moreover only esoteric theses can satisfy the imperious logical needs created by the philosophic and scientific positions of the modern world . . . Only esoterism . . . can provide answers that are neither fragmentary nor compromised in advance by a denominational bias. Just as rationalism can remove faith, so esoterism can restore it.'[12]

In order to follow an esoteric path it is not necessary to make a quantitative study of the doctrine; it is enough to know the essentials, which are centred on the nature of God and the nature of man. The symbolism of the elementary numbers is always enlightening, and in this case it is the number three which holds, as it were, the keys to understanding the relationship between the Creator and His human image. The presence of certain triads in the world, such as that of the primary colours, is the proof of a triplicity in the Divine Nature Itself, the Supreme Archetype of all that exists. In *From the Divine to the Human*, Schuon dwells at some length on this triplicity which is nothing other than the Absolute Infinite Perfection of God Himself, these three supreme transcendences being the intrinsic dimensions of Divine Reality. Perfection is, as he remarks, 'the Sovereign Good'; and having reminded us of St Augustine's saying that 'the good tends essentially to communicate itself', he adds: 'As Sovereign Good, the Absolute-Infinite cannot not project the world.'[13] But he goes on to remind us that It remains in Itself totally unaffected by this projection: 'Being what it is, the Absolute cannot not be immutable, and It cannot not radiate. Immutability, or fidelity to itself; and Radiation, or gift of Itself; there lies the essence of all that is.'[14]

[12] Frithjof Schuon, *Esoterism as Principle and as Way*, pp.7–8.

[13] This same truth is expressed in Islam as the already quoted tradition: 'I was a hidden treasure, and I loved to be known, and so I created the world.'

[14] p.42.

The Absolute Infinite Perfection is One. It transcends all multiplicity while being its root, and it is only at a lower level that we can begin to differentiate between the three terms of the triad. This is the level of what Schuon has called 'the relative Absolute'—a term which is applicable to the Christian Trinity and to Hinduism's analogous ternary Being-Consciousness-Beatitude.[15] At the same level, in Jewish and Islamic doctrine, are the non-essential Divine names such as Creator, which already implies the duality Creator-creature. Without being as yet manifested, the 'Hidden Treasure' is on the way to manifesting Itself.

If the Good is that which is to be manifested or communicated, the means of radiation is derived from the Infinite. These two intrinsic aspects of Reality are reflected by the Second and Third Persons of the Trinity, and, for Hinduism, by the corresponding Consciousness and Beatitude. 'It could be asked what relationship there is between the Good and Consciousness (*Chit*); now the Good, from the moment that It springs as such from the Absolute—which contains It in an undifferentiated or indeterminate manner—coincides with the distinctive Consciousness which the Absolute has of Itself; the Divine Word, which is the "Knowledge" that God has of Himself, cannot but be the Good, God being able to know Himself as Good only.'[16]

The Divine triplicity is reflected throughout the Universe in innumerable ways,[17] being especially intense in man himself. 'Man, "made in the image of God", has an intelligence capable of discernment and contemplation; a will capable of freedom and strength; a soul, or a character, capable of love and virtue.'[18] In the

[15] *Sat-Chit-Ānanda.*

[16] Ibid. p.39.

[17] Since the primary colours have been mentioned, we may say, in passing, that it is the right of the Absolute that we should know which is its colour before we have time to think. As to the Infinite, its right is, with regard to the same question, that our thoughts should unfold in the direction of its two great earthly symbols, the sky and the ocean. Nor is it difficult to see that Perfection, the Sovereign Good, is the Supreme Archetype of gold.

[18] Frithjof Schuon, *Esoterism as Principle and as Way*, p.101.

light of the quotation which precedes this, it is clear that intelligence corresponds to Perfection, the Sovereign Good. The same applies to doctrine, the content of the intelligence; all theology derives from the Divine Perfection by way of the Divine Word. Will and soul are rooted in the Absolute and the Infinite respectively. The psychic substance is the 'space' in which man deploys his faculties, and the primordial soul is no less than a vast presence. As to the primordial will—the will that is 'for God' in the most powerful sense of these words—it is irresistibly overwhelming:[19] no obstacle can stand in its way.

'Man may know, will and love; and to will is to act. We know God by distinguishing Him from whatever is not He and by recognizing Him in whatever bears witness to Him; we will God by accomplishing whatever leads us to Him and by abstaining from whatever removes us from Him; and we love God by Loving to know and to will Him, and by loving whatever bears witness to Him, around us as well as within us.'[20]

Man's three faculties, intelligence, will and soul, thus correspond to the equally interdependent ternary of doctrine, method, morals, or faith, practice, virtue, or 'comprehension concentration,[21] conformation'. It follows from the above quotations that to be effective the doctrine's initial appeal to the intelligence must include within its scope also the will and the soul. There can be no spirituality—or in other words no microcosm worthy of the name—without wholeness, that is, without sincerity, which means the harmonious co-operation of all these three faculties towards the common end. Nor indeed can there be any advance

[19] Even when perverted, the will retains something of the imprint of the Absolute, whence the terrible dangers inherent in ambition.

[20] Ibid. pp.95–6.

[21] The quintessence of esoteric practice is concentration on the Real. One of the most direct methodic supports for this is the invocation of the Divine Name, an orison said by Hinduism to be, for the whole of the Dark Age, the greatest means of Deliverance (*moksha*) and thus of Union (*yoga*) with the Divine Self, the One Real 'I' of which all subjectivities are reflections.

upon the esoteric way if the truth that is addressed to the mind does not lead to practice, and if both are not supported by virtue.

'Obviously the most brilliant intellectual knowledge is fruitless in the absence of the realising initiative that corresponds to it and in the absence of the necessary virtue; in other words, knowledge is nothing if it is combined with spiritual laziness and with pretensions, egoism, hypocrisy. Likewise the most prestigious power of concentration is nothing if it is accompanied by doctrinal ignorance and moral insufficiency; likewise again, natural virtue is but little without the doctrinal truth and the spiritual practice which operate it with a view to God and which thus restore to it the whole point of its being.'[22]

The movement towards the inward, which we are considering here may be said to represent the highest aspect of the extreme old age of the macrocosm. As such, in virtue of all that the times stand for in a positive sense, the esoterism in question could not be other than what the Hindus call *jnāna-marga*, the way of knowledge or, more precisely, of gnosis. It was fated to be so, for such a way presupposes a perspective of truth rather than love,[23] and it is objective regard for truth which characterizes the wisdom of old age.[24] It is beyond doubt significant in this respect that the last religion of the cycle, Islam—and therefore Sufism its esoteric dimension—should be dominated by the perspective of truth.

The mention of *jnāna* does not necessarily mean, in this context, a movement towards Hinduism. For each seeker the way in question could be, in principle, any one of the orthodox esoteric paths which are now operative. But before a way can be followed

[22] Ibid, p.169.

[23] Needless to say, it is not a question of mutually exclusive alternatives but of emphasis. Both elements must be present in every spiritual path.

[24] Even the many pseudo-esoterisms with which the modern age is rife purport to be ways of knowledge, no doubt in the awareness that otherwise they would be without attraction for contemporary seekers.

there must be an aspiration, and the word 'movement' is used here to mean the initial setting in motion of individuals in search of spiritual guidance and not the way itself, though this is bound to follow if the aspiration be a true one.

The seeming paradoxes and contradictions of our day are perhaps nowhere more apparent than in the literature of this most literate of all ages. On the one hand, like an old man who has become irrepressibly garrulous in his senility, the human race produces a ceaseless flow of books, and we may be certain that incomparably more is written than what reaches the stage of print. No period of history can come near to competing with this output either in terms of quantity or in terms of profanity and pointlessness—lack of the sense of reality, one might say. Most of these writings are in fact without pretension, for they claim to be no more than a means of lightly passing the day, and they have little hope of not being quickly superseded by others of their kind. They share with the mass media the blame of distracting man from the essential,[25] but they are far less dangerous than the writings of those literary, philosophic and scientific 'heroes' of the hour which serve to indoctrinate their readers with error in various forms and in general to imprison them within the limitations of the modern outlook.

At the same time, there are those many publications which reflect the already referred to archival aspect of finality. A general sense of the need to place everything on record—a sense that seems to be more collective than individual—has brought forth not only a spate of encyclopaedias but also a wealth of translations. The labour involved in making these records is for the most part no more than a passive participation in the wisdom of the age. The

[25] There is also the blame of modern man's lack of sense of royal responsibility for his vegetable kingdom. It has been calculated that about 15,000 fine forest trees are cut down to make enough paper to publish one issue only of one of the leading New York daily newspapers, almost all of which is thrown away the next day as rubbish.

motives are largely academic; but some of the classics[26] in question are of great spiritual value, and their present availability is a providential setting for those twentieth century works which may be considered as actively and centrally representative of our day in its best aspect,[27] and which no other age could have produced.

Amongst these signs of the times we will mention first of all *Man and his Becoming according to the Vedānta*[28] by René Guénon. As the title suggests, this book is a definition, in Hindu terms, of the whole nature of man and of the supreme spiritual possibilities which lie open to him. Although the author himself had already found a spiritual path in the esoterism of Islam, that is, in Sufism, he preferred, with characteristically impersonal reckoning, to take as the basis for his exposition something still further removed from Christianity than just another monotheism. This does not however prevent him from continually referring to the three Abrahamic traditions. It is significant, in view of what was cyclically needed, that the Advaita Vedānta has the advantage, shown by its altogether direct manner of expression, of never having had to speak in veiled terms in order to avoid a conflict with the limitations of exoterism. Moreover, as we have already seen, Hinduism possesses, like other religions of antiquity, the full doctrine of the *samsara*: it does not simplify the multiple reality of the great round of innumerable states of individual existence by narrowing it down to this one state of earthly life.

Another advantage of Hinduism as a basis for the exposition of universal truth is the comprehensive breadth of its structure. On the one hand, like Judaism and Islam, it depends on direct

[26] One of the first examples that comes to mind is *Hônen, the Buddhist Saint* by Shunjô.

[27] It is indeed ironical that the true nature of our times should so completely elude the comprehension of the most ardent champions of the twentieth century, including all those would-be artists, a majority alas, who are exclusively bent on producing works that reflect the age we live in. Instead of seeing a husk of decrepitude which envelops a luminous kernel of wisdom—and it is the kernel that any true art of our day would reflect—they see only the husk, which they refuse to recognize as such. There is no need to dwell on the result.

[28] *L'Homme et son devenir selon la Vêdânta*, first published in 1925.

revelation and makes a rigorous distinction between what is revealed and what is merely inspired. On the other hand, like Christianity, it depends on the Avatāra, that is, the descent of the Divinity into this world; and for the maintenance of the tradition there is a succession of no less than ten Avatāras. As far as historic times are concerned, the seventh and eighth of these, Rama and Krishna, are the most important for Hinduism itself. The ninth, specifically non-Hindu (literally 'foreign'), is generally considered to be the Buddha; and the tenth, Kalki, 'the rider on the white horse', will have the universal function of closing this cycle of time and inaugurating the next, which identifies his descent with the second advent of Christ.

Hinduism's breadth of structure is matched by its unequalled length of span across the centuries as a fully valid way of worship, by reason of its providential escape from the degeneracy which other religions of its own age suffered in the normal course. This brings us to the Aryan affinity which it has with the Western world as a whole. The fact that European languages are Indo-Germanic and therefore cognate with Sanskrit means, at a deeper level, that the religions of the ancient Greeks, Romans, Germans and Celts must have been originally so many counterparts or parallels of Hinduism. To make this most ancient religion the basis of a doctrinal exposition is thus to offer the Western world, for those few who are capable of taking it, a mysterious and purely positive renaissance of a relatively primordial heritage which has long been out of reach.

This question of affinity must not however be exaggerated. It means that there may be something in the European soul which is naturally open to the voice of Hinduism and predisposed to listen to its altogether objective approach to the doctrine. But it cannot be considered in a more operative sense, nor had Guénon any intention along those lines.[29] The great purpose behind *Man and*

[29] In letters to those who asked his advice—for he kept up a wide correspondence—he

his Becoming and all his other writings is to open his readers to the possibility of following an esoteric path, a possibility which, in the case of vocation becomes a necessity; but he does not recommend any one traditional line more than another. His motto was expressly *Vincit omnia veritas* 'Truth conquers all'; it was also, in fact, 'Seek and ye shall find' and 'Knock and it shall be opened unto you'. Implicit in his writings is the certainty of their author that they will providentially come to the notice of those qualified to receive his message, which will prove irresistible to them in the sense that they will be compelled to seek, and thus to find, a spiritual path. His books and articles are therefore, in intention and in fact, a treasury of information about what an intellectual—or one who is virtually so—needs to be made aware of; and a feature of Guénon's greatness is his remarkable grasp of the twentieth-century situation and his consequent ability to put his finger on the crucial gaps in modern man's understanding.

One of these gaps is the already mentioned failure to make a rigorous distinction between Intellect and reason, a distinction which he frequently emphasizes. Moreover to read the main part of his writing is to study metaphysics, which is concerned with the whole hierarchy of those states of being which transcend the human state, including those which transcend creation itself. One of his definitions of the qualification to follow an esoteric path is 'having the presentiment of one's higher states', which clearly takes us beyond the rational or mental domain.

Guénon is also an unsurpassed master of the science of symbolism, and a whole section of his work is devoted to that theme. The consciousness that the fabric of this world is woven out of symbols is not something that modern man acquires in the course of his education; and another closely related gap in his understanding has to do with the performance of sacred rites

tended to be discouraging with regard to Hinduism as a possible spiritual path for the Western seeker.

which are symbols enacted. The relationship between rite and symbol, at the best only partially understood, needed to be explained in greater depth. The following passages, from a chapter entitled 'The Language of the Birds', are representive of Guénon in more ways than one.

'There is often mention, in different traditions, of a mysterious language called "the language of the birds". The expression is clearly a symbolic one since the very importance which is attached to the knowledge of the language—it is considered to be the prerogative of a high initiation—precludes a literal interpretation. The Qur'ān for example says (XXVII, 15): "And Solomon was David's heir and he said: O men we have been taught the language of the birds, and all favours have been showered upon us." Elsewhere we read of heroes, like Siegfried in the Nordic legend, who understand the language of the birds as soon as they have overcome the dragon, and the symbolism in question may easily be understood from this. Victory over the dragon has, as its immediate consequence, the conquest of immortality which is represented by some object, the approach to which is barred by the dragon, and the conquest of immortality implies, essentially, reintegration at the centre of the human state, that is, at the point where communication is established with the higher states of the being. It is this communication which is represented by the understanding of the language of the birds and, in fact, birds are often taken to symbolise the angels and thus, precisely, the higher states. That is the significance, in the Gospel parable of the grain of mustard seed, of "the birds of the air" which came to lodge in the branches of the tree—the tree which represents the axis that passes through the centre of each state of being and connects all the states with each other. In the mediaeval symbol of the Peridexion (a corruption of *Paradision*) one sees birds on the branches of a tree and a dragon at its foot.'[30]

In the same article Guénon says, in speaking of the rhythmic

[30] *Fundamental Symbols*, p. 39.

formulae which are termed *dhikr*[31] in Sufism and *mantra* in Hinduism: 'The repetition of these formulae is intended to bring about the harmonization of the different elements of the being and to cause vibrations which, by their repercussions throughout the whole hierarchy of the states, are capable of opening up a communication with the higher states. This is moreover, generally speaking, the essential and primordial purpose of all rites.'[32] Elsewhere he says: 'Rite and symbol are basically two aspects of the same reality, namely the correspondence[33] which connects with each other all the degrees of universal existence. Through this correspondence, our human state can be put in communication with the higher states of the being.'[34]

One of the points which is especially stressed by Guénon is the need for the rite of initiation, without which there can be no question of an esoteric path. What is generally known in the West as 'the chain of apostolic succession' is merely one example, in a relatively outward domain, of something which all esoterisms have in common. The initiatic rite serves to attach fallen man, through the chain which goes back to the founder of the religion himself, to a new ancestral line. Without this true and effective renewal of primordial heredity, there could be no hope of regaining one's first nature, except by a miracle which no one has the right to expect, least of all one who had had the presumption to refuse to follow the normal course.

In addition to his writings on esoterism, Guénon also wrote books which are mainly concerned with the errors of the modern world,[35] though here also esoterism is always present in the back-

[31] Literally 'remembrance', which must be understood in the light of what has already been said about 'Platonic remembrance' with regard to the power of the symbol to recall its archetype.

[32] Ibid. p.40.

[33] He means the symbol–archetype correspondence.

[34] *Aperçus sur l'initiation*, p.122.

[35] *The Crisis of the Modern World*, for example and *The Reign of Quantity and the Signs of the Times*.

ground as 'the one thing necessary', the indispensable corner-stone for any restoration of the world to normality. A note which is sounded in all his writings is the need for orthodoxy, a term which has become, in academic use, almost a synonym for narrow and fanatical exoterism, but which Guénon re-establishes in its true sense, while extending its guarantee of rightness beyond the limits of one religion only. In his perspective it takes on a vast significance, to include, for all seekers of religious truth, every form of worship that has its origin in Divine intervention and has been faithfully transmitted from generation to generation by an uninterrupted process of tradition.

With Guénon mention must also be made of Ananda Coomaraswamy.[36] In most respects they cover the same ground, for the writings of both are centred on metaphysical principles and both, from this same standpoint, wrote pertinent and devastating criticisms of the modern world. In particular Coomaraswamy was also, like Guénon, a master of symbolism; but there is a whole aesthetic dimension in Coomaraswamy that is lacking in Guénon, who was not an authority on art. Needless to say, it is their similarities rather than their differences which bring them into the present context; but within the general framework of terminal wisdom, it cannot be denied that there is a certain complementary relationship between the two.[37]

A typical example of Coomaraswamy's writing is his article 'Symplegades', so entitled because its starting point is 'The

[36] Coomaraswamy's *The Bugbear of Literacy* is an example which may be added to the two books of Guénon mentioned in the previous note. Ananda is not to be confused with his son Rama, whose recent book *The Destruction of the Christian Tradition* has been quoted in an earlier chapter.

[37] This is well brought out in the A.K. Coomaraswamy Centenary Issue of *Studies in Comparative Religion* (Summer, 1977), in the article 'Coomaraswamy: the Man, Myth and History' by Whitall Perry, whose monumental *A Treasury of Traditional Wisdom* may be mentioned here as another of those works which only this age could have produced. Its undertaking was inspired, so the author tells us, by Coomaraswamy's remark. 'The time is coming when a Summa of the Philosophia Perennis will have to be written, impartially based on all orthodox sources whatsoever.'

Clashing Rocks' of Greek mythology. These rocks have, as he shows, many different parallels in other traditions, in particular the various forms of 'The Active Door', that is, the gateway through which it is difficult and dangerous to pass because the two leaves of the portal, in some cases represented as 'razor-edged', are liable to snap suddenly together. This side of the 'narrow gate' is the domain of earthly nature and of man; beyond it lies the Transcendent. Sometimes the passage is made in order to bring a celestial object to earth as when, for the quest of the Golden Fleece, Jason's boat Argo is driven by Athene, Goddess of Wisdom, between the Clashing Rocks which she holds apart. More often however it is a question of the spiritual path of no return, and of the passage from mortality to Immortality. But in any case, none can pass safely between the rocks or the door-leaves by merely human resource. Divine aid is needed—for example, a God-given incantation or invocation. In some Eskimo legends the souls of men are represented by birds, in particular geese migrating to the South at the onset of Winter, and it is only 'the fast fliers' (that is, as Coomaraswamy remarks, those who have duly received initiation, the mandate of Heaven) who escape being crushed to death by 'the clapping mountains' which are a form of 'the clashing rocks'. Another form is that of 'the clashing waters', if the Exodus be interpreted in its esoteric sense, 'the crossing of the Red Sea from the Egyptian darkness of this world to a Promised Land'. Yet another form, to be found in a Greenland myth, is that of 'two clashing icebergs'.

The Symplegades have also a temporal significance: 'An unmistakable reference to the Clashing Rocks is to be found in Rgveda, VI, 49.3, where the 'Rocks' are times, viz., Day and Night, described as "clashing together and parting"'. He quotes also from the *Kanṣītaki Brāhmana*: 'Night and Day are the Sea that carries all away, and the two Twilights are its fordable crossings; so he sacrifices [performs the sacrifice to Agni] at Twilight . . . Night and Day, again, are the encircling arms of Death; and just as a man about to grasp you with both arms can be escaped through the opening between them, so he sacrifices at Twilight . . . this is the sign of the Way-of-the-Gods, which he takes hold of, and safely reaches Heaven.'

Coomaraswamy gives far more examples than those few mentioned here; and while basing his exposition mainly on the sacred books of Hinduism, he quotes also copiously from an immense variety of other sources, Buddhist, American Indian, Jewish, Pythagorean, Hermetic, Platonic and Neo-Platonic, Christian,[38] and Islamic, with additional references to world-wide 'folklore' survivals from more ancient traditions.

In conclusion he says: 'It remains only to consider the full doctrinal significance of the Symplegades. What the formula states literally is that whoever would transfer from this to the Otherworld, or return, must do so through the undimensioned and timeless "interval" that divides related but contrary forces, between which, if one is to pass at all, it must be "instantly" . . . It is, then precisely from these "pairs" that liberation must be won, from their conflict that we must escape, if we are to be freed from our mortality . . . Here, under the Sun, we are "overcome by the pairs" (*Maitri Upanishad* III, 1): here "every being in the emanated-world moves deluded by the mirage of the contrary-pairs, of which the origin is in our liking and disliking . . . but those who are freed from this delusion of the pairs . . . freed from the pairs that are implied by the expression 'weal and woe', these reach the place of invariability" (*Bhagavad Gītā* VII, 27-8 and XV, 5).' He adds, from St Nicholas of Cusa: 'The wall of the Paradise in which Thou, Lord dwellest, is built of contradictories, nor is there any way to enter but for one who has overcome the highest Spirit of Reason[39] who guards its gate (*De Visione Dei*, chapter IX, to end)'.

[38] The Christian sources include Dionysus, St Augustine, St Thomas Aquinas, Dante, Eckhardt, Ruysbroeck, St Nicholas of Cusa, Boehme and Angelus Silesius, not to mention numerous references to the mediaeval romances of Chrétien de Troyes and others.

[39] The plane of reason is, precisely, the plane of opposites, and to overcome the one is to overcome the other. But this can only be achieved by the Intellect which is suprarational

These paragraphs will at least serve to give some inkling of the great interest of this article in itself, which 'proves' the existence of a universal consciousness, going back to incalculably early times, of the need to transcend our human state, and of the impossibility of doing so without the help of the Transcendent, the 'mandate of Heaven'. 'Symplegades' is moreover merely one example amongst many others which display the same qualities. Again and again Coomaraswamy goes out to meet the modern world's so-called intelligentsia on their own ground, that is, the ground of what they would call 'purely objective scholarship', which alone they respect. It is as if he had said: 'You ask for scholarship and nothing but that, so let us have it; but let it be the real thing, in fullness and in depth, not merely a surface smattering.' Having thus as it were thrown down the gauntlet, he takes some theme of basic importance for religion in general and proceeds to expound his thesis with a mastery which no modern authority of learning could fail to recognize—we might even say, at which no such authority could fail to feel dwarfed, for the writings of Coomaraswamy have evoked in many minds, both before and since his death in 1947, the question as to whether any other equally great scholar has ever existed. However that may be, his books and articles demonstrate amongst other things that beneath the superficial differences and apparent contradictions at which most modernist minds tend to stop short, there lies a complete traditional unanimity the world over for all that is of essential significance, a unanimity of far-reaching implications which cannot be disregarded.

If we were to sum up the work of Coomaraswamy as 'truth', that of Guénon could be summed up with the word 'orthodoxy'. In reading Guénon we are scarcely ever allowed to lose sight of the driving force behind his pen, the already mentioned purpose or hope of enabling and impelling a qualified minority to take effective spiritual action. This purpose was no doubt also present

---

and, in its highest reaches, Divine, and which alone can conquer the dualism to which man became subject through eating the fruit of the forbidden tree.

in Coomaraswamy, but the reader is less aware of it. One's immediate impression is of a vast canvas of metaphysical and cosmological truth which stretches the intelligence towards its limits, enlarging it and enlightening it, and thus predisposing it for the spiritual work which is the methodic complement of doctrine—a complement which tends to be no more than implicit in Coomaraswamy, whereas in Guénon it is altogether explicit.

The mention of these two writers recalls the great commandment: 'Thou shalt love the Lord thy God with all thy Heart, and with all thy soul, and with all thy mind, and with all thy strength'.[40] It was part of their function to recall the forgotten truth, affirmed by traditions all over the world, that the Heart is the throne of the Intellect. As to the rest of the commandment, the tendency of Western religious authorities in recent centuries had been to sacrifice almost totally 'with all thy mind' for the supposed benefit of 'with all thy soul' and 'with all thy strength'. In consequence, piety had become more and more sentimental, and minds, set free for other things, had worked themselves up into an unparalleled state of unrest. The modern civilization is largely the result. But it has been the function of Guénon and Coomaraswamy to recall some minds from the profane to the sacred, and to awaken others which were half asleep for want of a true object. The writings of these two sages, which could not have been expected by any chain of worldly causality, are indeed so opportune as to be suggestive of something in the nature of a mission. This does not mean that we are claiming for either the status of prophethood, which both would have disclaimed. But it may none the less be relevant to remember, in connection with them, the promise contained in the closing words of the Old Testament: 'Behold I will send you Elijah the prophet before the coming of the great and dreadful day of the Lord: And he shall turn the heart of the fathers to the children, and the heart of the children to their fathers, lest I come and smite the earth with a curse'.[41]

[40] St Mark, XII, 30. [41] Malachi, IV, 5–6.

In connection with this passage, in an article about the function of Elijah—or Elias, as he is called in the New Testament—Leo Schaya remarks that the relationship between 'fathers' and 'children' signifies the 'tradition', the religious teaching which is passed from the one to the other. He adds: 'The "heart of the fathers" is the central inward aspect, the essence of the tradition, its esoteric spiritual and universal nucleus; it is also the doctrines, methods and influences which are derived from it. The "heart of the children" or believers is their spiritual receptivity, their inward acceptance and reception of what is given them by their "fathers" . . . This acceptance or reception is expressed in Hebrew by the word *Qabbalah* which has become synonymous quite specifically with the esoteric tradition in which Elias is the invisible Master, he who descends secretly to this lower world, not only towards the end but each time, ever since his ascension, that the tradition has needed reviving from within.'[42] Schaya also says: 'When he returns towards the end of time . . . Elias will raise his voice so loud, says Jewish tradition, that it will be heard from one end of the earth to the other. This means that Elias' mission is not confined to Israel, but will spread to all peoples and thereby to all religions'. The Gospel likewise reiterates the promise that Elias will come again before the end: 'Elias shall truly first come and restore all things'.[43] But Jesus adds that he has also already come in the person of John the Baptist; and Gabriel foretold to Zachariah that his son would proceed 'in the spirit and power of Elias'.[44] Schaya concludes: 'Elias therefore means not only a prophet sent to Israel but also a universal function which may be exercised by several persons both within Judaism and within other traditions.'

We will come back later to the question of Elias. Meantime he has been mentioned here because the works of Guénon and Coomaraswamy are precisely, in a very full sense, a turning of 'the

[42] 'The Eliatic Function' in *Studies in Comparative Religion*, Winter-Spring, 1979, p.15.

[43] St Matthew, XVII, 11.

[44] St Luke, I, 17.

heart of the fathers to the children' in order to operate a turning of the 'heart of the children to their fathers'. This, together with the almost prophetic suddenness of the Guénon-Coomaraswamy phenomenon, is a powerful indication that they were destined to inaugurate, for this cyclic moment, the workings of 'the Eliatic function'.

Their writing leads up to that of Frithjof Schuon. It could be said, again at the risk of simplification, that if Coomaraswamy represents truth in which commitment is implicit, and if Guénon represents both truth and commitment, it was left to Schuon to add his insistence on the need for total commitment, while at the same time, as regards doctrinal truth, his works are a self-sufficient whole. It could also be said that if the writings of Guénon lead to initiation, those of Schuon lead both to it and beyond it, for they contain a dimension of method which it was not the function of his two predecessors to give.

'Knowledge saves,' says Schuon, 'only on condition that it enlists all that we are: only when it is a way which tills and which transforms, and which wounds our nature as the plough wounds the earth . . .' Metaphysical knowledge is sacred. It is the right of sacred things to demand of man all that he is.'[45]

It was necessary that Guénon and Coomaraswamy should do concentrated justice to 'with all thy mind', and this they did, even to the point of partially neglecting 'with all thy soul'. Some enthusiasts of Guénon have wrongly concluded from his works that the whole esoteric path depends on the assimilation of doctrine and the correct performance of orthodox rites, and on nothing else, as if the virtues were not also essential. Guénon himself, if asked, would certainly have affirmed their necessity. His avoidance of the moral issue may have been deliberate, in view of a generation in full reaction against unintelligent moralism. However this may be, the reaction none the less called for an answer; and Schuon gives it by speaking of the moral dimension in a new,

[45] *Spiritual Perspectives and Human Facts*, pp.144–5.

unmoralistic and more intellectually convincing way, with a stress on the importance of outward beauty, whether it be of nature or of art, as a prolongation of the inward beauty of virtue. In general the absence of the element 'with all thy soul' in Guénon and Coomaraswamy may not be unconnected with the extreme objectivity of their writings which was carried to the point of excluding any intrusion of their own individualities into what they wrote. Schuon is no less objective, where objectivity is required, than they are; but in reading him, one is conscious of a subject that is adequate to the cyclic significance of the writing itself. Nor can it be doubted that the living inwardness which penetrates his works does much to bestow on them their remarkable, integrating power—the power to draw both the mind and the soul in the direction of the Heart.

To the many quotations already made from Schuon throughout this book we will simply add here a paragraph which is particularly relevant to our immediate context: 'The virtues, which by their very nature bear witness to the Truth also possess an interiorising quality according to the measure in which they are fundamental; the same is true of beings and things that transmit the messages of eternal Beauty; whence the power of interiorisation that belongs to virgin nature, to the harmony of creatures, to sacred art, to music . . . If we wish to withdraw into the Heart in order to find there the total Truth and the underlying pre-personal Holiness, we must manifest the Heart not only in our intelligence but also in our soul in general, by means of spiritual attitudes and moral qualities; for every beauty of the soul is a ray coming from the Heart and leading back to it.'[46]

As is clear from its title, the recent work from which these words are taken has a very direct bearing on the theme of this chapter. We have added, as an appendix,[47] some reflections on his equally relevant *Sufism: Veil and Quintessence*. But his other

[46] *Esoterism as Principle and as Way*, p.234.

[47] Appendix A.

writings[48] are no less fully representative of the spirit of the times. On the one hand we are conscious of all those positive qualities which belong to the end of an age, in particular of a supreme mastery of summing up and of putting everything in its right place. Again and again, about this or about that, one has the impression that Schuon has said the last word. On the other hand we are conscious of the meeting of extremes and of a light that is primordial as well as terminal.

[48] All those available in English are listed under his name in the bibliography.

6

The Restorer

It is not given to man to foresee the future with any clarity—otherwise prophecies would be neither veiled nor ambiguous. But man has the right to speculate about the future in humble awareness of his limitations in that respect—otherwise prophecies would not be forthcoming at all. Moreover in some cases a settled conviction is legitimate and even, we may say, willed by Heaven, in virtue of the weight and universality of the predictions; and so it is with regard to an imminent world-wide devastation, not total, but none the less of cataclysmic proportions, and not final, because it is to be 'before the end', though there are grounds for conviction that 'the end' itself cannot be far off.

The predictions leave no doubt as to the cause of such a Divine intervention; and enough has already been said to show that a large section of humanity has now reached an extreme of error beyond which it would be difficult to go. But the error could never have become universal, for the macrocosm, taken as a whole, is a sacred thing. Like all that is relative, it has to confess its relativity in the face of the Absolute, which it does by suffering a Dark Age, that is, by growing old. But it is not conceivable that it could ever be deserted by Heaven. Like the true microcosm, the macrocosm is a norm, and as such it has its rights: amongst these is the right to be protected against the errors of man; and the human race, which in itself may be considered as macrocosm, has the right to be protected against those of mankind who have rejected their humanity by refusing to conform to the human function.

Of all communities now living, it is probably the American Indians who are, thanks to their traditional way of life, the most sensitive to the sanctity of the macrocosm. By them, in consequence, the vast destruction which they believe to be at hand is seen in a purely positive light, as a normalizing act of Heaven that will obliterate all the erections with which man has disfigured and desecrated the holy face of earth—whence the term Purification Day which for them designates this long awaited event. In Islam also the event is predicted in terms which the Indians would find reassuring. Nor need this surprise us, despite the many differences between the two perspectives in question, for Islam has always remained deeply conscious of its nomadic origins. It has moreover a double right to its claim of primordiality, one in retrospect, as a return to the pre-Judaic religion of Abraham, and the other by anticipation in virtue of its place at the threshold of the new primordial age. The Qur'ān states specifically that before the end every town shall be either totally destroyed or severely punished;[1] and it may be assumed that this will have been preceded by a frenzy of urbanism, for when asked about the signs that would herald the approach of the latter days, the Prophet made mention in particular of the excessive height of the buildings that men would build.[2]

The term Purification Day suggests a possibility of redress before the close of the cycle; and in the Gospel account of the period which precedes the end there is likewise an element which, amidst all the evils explicitly foretold, might seem to imply reason for hope. Christ spoke of calamity after calamity, leading down to 'great tribulation such as was not since the beginning of the world'. Then he added the already quoted words: 'And except those days should be shortened, there should be no flesh saved:

[1] XVII, 58.

[2] See Martin Lings, *Muhammad: His Life Based on the Earliest Sources*, pp.330–1.

but for the elect's sake those days shall be shortened.'[3] The verses which immediately follow are as negative as those which precede, and they are usually taken to refer to the Antichrist. But the shortening of the days for the sake of the elect suggests that after the destruction the elect may be able to achieve something, if only for a while;[4] and in this more positive context we may refer back to the Old Testament promise that Elijah will come again before the end. Particularly relevant also is the wording of the promise of Jesus: 'Elias shall truly first come and restore all things'.

In Islam the restorer is mentioned in many sayings of the Prophet. Without being named, he is referred to as 'the rightly guided one', *al-Mahdī*; and it may be presumed, in view of the vast scope of his authority, that the coming of the Mahdi will mark the fulfilment of the Jewish and Christian Eliatic hopes.[5] The Islamic traditions point to a world-wide function which, although situated in Islam, is of too universal a nature not to extend beyond its boundaries, at least by radiation if not by deliberate and mandated action. Nor can it be excluded that redresses which are now impossible the world over might become, under his aegis, once more possible outside Islam as well as within it, after a 'Purification Day' had removed the obstacles. It was with reference to the preliminary redress to be effected by the Mahdi in anticipation of the total Messianic redress that Guénon wrote the following passage: 'For that (total) redress the way will have to be prepared, even visibly, before the end of the present cycle; but this can only be done by him who unites in himself the forces of Heaven and

[3] See p.11–12.

[4] In her third apparition to the children of Fatima, the Blessed Virgin said, in speaking of the destruction: 'Some nations will be annihilated. But in the end, my Immaculate Heart will triumph. The Holy Father will consecrate Russia to me, and she will be converted, and a period of peace will be granted to the world.' (*Fatima in Lucia's Own Words*, p.162. See also John de Marchi, *Fatima from the Beginning*, p.79.) Some have sensed a prediction of peace also in St Malachy's prophecy of the popes (see p.129), in relation to the next pope, whose reign is therein designated 'the glory of the olive' (*gloria olivae*).

[5] For a more detailed identification of the Mahdi with Elias, see Leo Schaya, *The Eliatic Function*, pp.36–8.

Earth, of the East and the West, and who shall manifest in the domains both of knowledge and of action the two-fold power of priest and of king which has been preserved throughout the ages in the integrity of its one principle.'[6]

The hopeful expectation of the Mahdi has produced in Islam a number of false Mahdis throughout the centuries. Of the true Mahdi the Prophet said: 'He will be broad of forehead and aquiline of nose. He will fill the earth with right and with justice even as it hath been filled with wrong and oppression. Seven years will he reign.' But towards the end of his reign or after it, Islam expects also the Antichrist. The Prophet is said to have mentioned that many had already foretold the coming of this greatest of evils, but that he himself was the first to make known a clear bodily sign by which he might be recognized. He would be 'a man blind in his right eye, in which all light is extinguished, even as it were a grape'. As in Christianity, it is believed in Islam that he will cause corruption, and that by his power to work marvels he will win many to his side. But he will none the less be resisted. The Prophet said: 'A body of my people will not cease to fight for the truth until the coming forth of the Antichrist'; and he meant this inclusively, as shown by what he says of the resistance to the Antichrist 'When they are pressing on to fight, even while they straighten their lines for the prayer when it is called, Jesus the son of Mary will descend and will lead them in prayer. And the enemy of God, when he seeth Jesus, will melt even as salt melteth in water. If he were let be, he would melt into perishing: but God will slay him at the hand of Jesus, who will show them his blood upon his lance.'

The explanation of the almost simultaneous presence of the Mahdi and the Antichrist will already be clear from the last chapter. The two opposite tendencies which, as we have seen, inevitably characterize the end of the cycle reach their extreme of

[6] *Aperçus sur l'initiation*, p.264. The chapter in question was first published as an article, 'Initiation sacerdotale et initiation royale', in *Le Voile d'Isis*, 1931, the French journal which later became *Etudes Traditionnelles*.

opposition in these two beings. It is the Mahdi who incarnates 'the spirit of the times'; but the macrocosm has to die, and the Antichrist is its final and fatal sickness. As to those who personify its terminal wisdom, above all the Mahdi and, with him, the elect, they may thereby also be considered as the providential receptacles for the light which shines into the end of this cycle from the outset of the next. It is thus that although the Antichrist is said to come after the Mahdi or towards the end of his reign, spreading corruption and partly undoing his work, the Mahdi is none the less he who will have the last word, inasmuch as his kingdom is the harbinger of the new age, wherein it will have its prolongation, after having displayed in itself its own perfection of maturity and fulfilment.

APPENDIX A

On *Sufism: Veil and Quintessence* by Frithjof Schuon

The preface opens with an explanation of the title: the 'Veil' is the opaqueness which is given off by pious extravagances of expression. The first chapter, 'Ellipsis and Hyperbole in Arab Rhetoric', puts before us many examples of those kinds of incoherence which all too often obscure Sufism's quintessence. One of the most striking features of the earlier parts of this book is the profound and subtle analysis of the type of soul which tends to generate the veils, and of the complementary type which reacts against them. Schuon's understanding of racial differences has been displayed in his *Castes and Races*. But in this new book he concentrates on one race alone, dwelling on the differences between its two main branches.

Although it could be said that every esoterism in the full sense of the word is universal, there are none the less affinities to be considered. Sufism, as the last esoterism of this cycle of time, cannot fail to have a certain temporal affinity with men of today. But there is also a racial factor to be considered, for although Sufism has become widely operative amongst yellow and black race communities, it cannot be said to owe them any of its basic characteristics. Paradoxically this does not prevent it from being in fact more easily accessible to some sectors of these races than it is to the modem Westerner. But that has nothing to do with racial affinity; it is merely that the communities in question are less firmly rooted in the totally profane and therefore anti-esoteric civilization which dominates the West. The fact remains that Sufism is an esoterism of the white race, if it be permissible to say such a thing; and herein lies one of the reasons why this book is of vital importance; for although the double claim of Sufism is bound, in the nature of things, to remain entirely virtual for the vast majority of Westerners now living, it is urgent that all outward and as it were accidental barriers between it and the West should be eliminated. Because of these 'veils', a man might say: 'Sufism is not for me', when it might be the very thing he needed most of all.

Europeans and their offshoots in other parts of the world have long been aware of two hereditary strains within them. Matthew Arnold, for example, was acutely conscious of two influences, complementary or conflicting, in English literature, and he termed them Hebraism and Hellenism. Schuon takes us more vastly and profoundly into this consciousness, and he needs for his purpose the wider terms of Semitism and Aryanism. The following passage makes us aware, from the start, of the complexity in question: 'Psychologically, there are "introverted" and contemplative Aryans, the Hindus, and "extroverted" and enterprising Aryans, the Europeans; East and West, with the obvious reservation that the characteristics of the one are also to be found in the other. In the case of the Semites, who on the whole are more contemplative than Europeans and less contemplative than Hindus, there are also two principal groups, Jews and Arabs: the soul of the former is richer[1] but more turned in on itself, while that of the latter is poorer[2] but more expansive, more gifted from the

[1] For a glimpse of this 'richness', one has only to read the biblical account of the building of the Temple in the early chapters of Chronicles II.

[2] In this connection, to avoid giving an oversimplified impression of what Schuon means, the following passages should also be quoted: 'No doubt the Arab soul has its richness—the contrary would be inconceivable—but it has a poor richness; or a poverty enriched by the scintillation of nomadic virtues, and enhanced by a so to speak desert-like acuteness of intelligence . . . If there is a poor richness, there is also, and not less paradoxically, a rich poverty, and it is this that predisposed the Arabs to Islam and, along with it,

point of view of radiance and universality.' The author adds, by way of a note: 'In this comparison we are thinking of orthodox Jews—those who have remained Orientals even in the West—and not of the totally Europeanized Jews, who combine certain Semitic characteristics with Western extroversion.'

Further light is thrown on the different types two paragraphs later: '*Grosso modo*, the Aryans—except in cases of intellectual obscuration in which they have only retained their mythology and ritualism—are above all metaphysicians and therefore logicians, whereas the Semites—if they have not become idolators and magicians—are *a priori* mystics and moralists; each of the two mentalities or capacities repeating itself within the framework of the other, in conformity with the Taoist symbol of the *yin-yang*. Or again, the Aryans are objectivists, for good or for ill, while the Semites are subjectivists; deviated objectivism gives rise to rationalism and scientism, whereas abusive subjectivism engenders all the illogicalities and all the pious absurdities of which sentimental fideism—over zealous and conventional—is capable.' Let us quote also a passage which shows as clearly as possible how far the scope of this book extends beyond the domain of the Hebraism-Hellenism contrast which we have, as it were, in our blood: 'The encounter of Hinduism and Islam on the soil of India has something profoundly symbolic and providential about it, given that Hinduism is the most ancient integral tradition and that Islam on the contrary is the youngest religion; it is the junction of the primordial with the terminal. But there is here more than a symbol; this encounter means in fact that each of these traditions, which are nevertheless as different as possible, has something to learn from the other, not of course from the point of view of dogmas and practices, but from that of tendencies and attitudes; Islam offers its geometric simplicity, its clarity

---

to a mysticism of holy poverty: the saint, in Islam, is the "one who is poor", the *faqīr*, and the spiritual virtue par excellence, which moreover coincides with sincerity (*ṣidq*), is "poverty", *faqr*.'

and also its compassion, while Hinduism brings its influence to bear by its profound serenity and by its multiform and inexhaustible universality.'

It will no doubt have been understood from what has already been said that the veils which are this book's preliminary theme may be said to result from the Semitic origins of Sufism, while Western reactions against them spring from our Aryan heredity. The reactions are no doubt all the stronger in that many of these Western readers who turn their attention to Sufism do so because they hope to find in it something they have failed to find in Christianity. The consciousness of this failure means that they have largely thrown off the Hebraism that the Bible had superimposed upon their Aryan roots. Their standpoint will therefore tend to be that of un-Semiticized Aryans.

Several aspects of veiling are treated in the book, with a wealth of illustration. The author speaks of his 'twofold obligation to criticize and to justify'. Without minimizing faults he explains how the fault in question comes to exist and what positive qualities lie at its roots. Also to be considered are the differences of approach which call for no criticism provided that they are innocent of intolerance and of exaggeration, but which none the less need to be explained. The following paragraph touches on points of the greatest practical importance and is instructive, in different ways, for both the Semite and the Aryan.

'A Westerner desirous of following an esoteric way would find it logical first of all to inform himself of the doctrine, then to enquire about the method and finally about its general conditions; but the Muslim of esoteric inclination—and the attitude of the Qabbalist is doubtless analogous—has definitely the opposite tendency: if one speaks to him of metaphysics, he will find it natural to reply that one must begin at the beginning, namely with pious exercises and all sorts of religious observances; metaphysics will be for later. He does not seem to realise that in the eyes of the Westerner, as also of the Hindu, this is to deprive the pious practices of their very point—not in themselves of course, but with a view to knowledge—and to make the way almost unintelligible; and above all, the Semitic zealot does not see that understanding of doctrine cannot result from a moral and individualistic zeal, but that on the contrary it is there to inaugurate a new dimension and to explain its nature and purpose. We may add that the moralistic attitude is only blameworthy through its ignorance of the opposite point of view or through its exaggeration, for in fact the doctrine deserves on our part an element of reverential fear; even our own spirit does not belong to us, and we only have full access to it to the extent that we know this. If it is true that the doctrine explains the meaning of devotion, it is equally true that devotion has a certain right to usher in the doctrine, and that the doctrine deserves this.'

Another kind of veil, not unrelated to those already mentioned, results from simplification. By way of example, Schuon shows that in their disagreements with the philosophers the Sufis have not always had right on their side. Let us quote what he says about the philosophers' claim that the world is eternal, and his re-formulation or correction of the Sufis' total and over simplified rejection of this: 'The world is both eternal and temporal: eternal as a series of creations or creative rhythm, and temporal by the fact that each link in this flux has a beginning and an end. It is Universal Manifestation in itself that is co-eternal with God because it is a necessary expression of His eternal Nature—the sun being unable to abstain from shining—but eternity cannot be reduced to a given contingent phase of this divine Manifestation. Manifestation is "co-eternal", that is: not eternal, as only the Essence is; and this is why it is periodically interrupted and totally re-absorbed into the Principle, so that it is both existent and inexistent, and does not enjoy a plenary and so to speak "continuous" reality like the Eternal itself.'

Let us also quote the following: 'In a certain respect, the difference between philosophy, theology and gnosis is total; in another respect, it is relative. It is total when one understands by "philosophy" only rationalism; by "theology", only the explanation of religious teachings; and by "gnosis", only intuitive and intellective, and thus supra-rational, knowledge; but the difference is only relative when one understands by "philosophy" the fact of thinking, by "theology" the fact of speaking dogmatically of God and religious things, and by "gnosis" the fact of presenting pure metaphysics, for then the *genres* interpenetrate. It is impossible to deny that the most illustrious Sufis, while being "gnostics" by definition, were at the same time to some extent theologians and to some extent philosophers, or that the great theologians were to some extent philosophers and to some extent gnostics, the last word having to be understood in its proper and non-sectarian meaning.'

The ground has now been cleared for what is the climax of the book, a chapter entitled 'The Quintessential Esoterism of Islam'. Although very concentrated, it is shorter than one might have expected, but this accords with the nature of the quintessence which is its theme. As the author remarks: 'To describe known or what one may call literary Sufism in all its *de facto* complexity and all its paradoxes would require a whole book, whereas to give an account of the necessary and therefore concise character of Sufism, a few pages can suffice.'

The contents of this chapter may surprise some readers owing to widespread fallacies about the true nature of esoterism. Other readers on the contrary will have been well prepared by the author's *Esoterism as Principle and as Way*, in which he states categorically: 'The profoundest truths are already given in the fundamental and initial formulations of the religions. Esoterism, in fact, is not an unpredictable doctrine that can only be discovered, should the occasion arise, by means of detailed researches; what is mysterious in esoterism is its dimension of depth, its particular developments, and its practical consequences, but not its starting points, which coincide with the basic symbols of the religion in question.'

It is therefore not surprising that the chapter should open with a reference to the three basic divisions of Islam: 'The Islamic religion is divided into three parts: *Īmān*, Faith, which contains everything one must believe; *Islām*, the Law, which contains everything one must do; *Iḥsān*, operative virtue, which confers upon believing and doing the qualities that make them perfect or, in other words, that intensify and deepen both faith and works. *Iḥsān*, in short, is the sincerity of the intelligence and the will: it is our adherence to the Truth and our total conformity to the Law, which means that we must, on the one hand, know the Truth entirely, not in part only, and on the other hand conform to it with our deepest being and not only with a partial and superficial will. Thus *Iḥsān* opens out into esoterism—which is the science of the essential and the total—and is even identical with it; for to be sincere is to draw from the Truth the maximal consequences from the point of view of both the intelligence and the will; in other words, it is to think and will with the heart, and thus with our whole being, with all that we are.'

This passage gives the key to the understanding of the whole, for it shows that Sufism, far from being other than Islam, is in fact total or absolute Islam as opposed to the fragmentary or relative Islam of exoterism. We are thus prepared in advance to read: 'The two-fold Testimony is the first and most important of the five "Pillars of the Religion". The others only have meaning in reference to it, and they are the following: Canonical Prayer; the Fast of Ramadan; Almsgiving; Pilgrimage. The esoterism of these practices resides not only in their obvious initiatic symbolism, it resides also in the fact that our practices are esoteric to the extent that we ourselves are esoteric, firstly by our understanding of the Doctrine and then by our assimilation of the Method; these two elements being contained, precisely, in the two-fold Testimony.'

The first formula of this Testimony is *lā ilāha illā Llāh*, 'there is no god but God', which can be paraphrased 'there is no reality but the (One) Reality'. Schuon explains in some detail how the whole doctrine of the Absolute and its manifestations is implicitly contained in this. More explicit is the second formula, *Muḥammadun Rasūlu Llāh*, Muhammad is the Messenger of God. 'The word *Rasūl*, "Messenger", indicates a "descent" of God towards the world; it also implies an "ascent" of man towards God . . . In the human microcosm the descent is inspiration, and the ascent is aspiration; the descent is Divine Grace, while the ascent is human effort, the content of which is "the remembrance of God" (*dhikru Llāh*), whence the name *Dhikru Llāh* given to the Prophet.' As to the other four pillars of Islam: 'Prayer marks the submission[3] of Manifestation to the Principle; the Fast is detachment with regard to desires, thus with regard to the ego; the Almsgiving is detachment with regard to things, thus with regard to the world; the Pilgrimage, finally, is the return to the Centre, to the Heart; to the Self. A sixth pillar is sometimes added, the Holy War: this is the fight against the profane soul by means of the spiritual weapon.'[4]

This chapter is centred on Absolute Oneness. It is fittingly followed by a complementary final chapter which is centred, implicitly, on Absolute Plenitude. Explicitly, it is on the three dimensions of Oneness which are expressed by the words Absolute Infinite Perfection, and which esoterism can never lose sight of. We first know these dimensions in their reflections on the plane of our earthly experience—or rather we recognize them as evident when Schuon points them out to us.

'God is manifested in the world, as we have said, by the miracle of existence, the gulf between the least grain of dust and nothingness being absolute; He manifests his Infinity *a priori* by the cosmic container space-time, which has no imaginable limits, any more than do the multiplicity and diversity of its contents; and

[3] The prayer culminates in the prostration which signifies, esoterically, the extinction (or reabsorption) of the relative in the Absolute, of the accident in the Substance.

[4] The chief spiritual weapon is *dhikru Llāh*, the remembrance of God which means, methodically speaking, the invocation of the Name *Allāh*.

He manifests His Perfection by the qualities of things and beings, which bear witness to their divine archetypes and thereby to the divine Perfection . . . On the one hand, space together with time, then the existence of things, and then their qualities, "prove" God; on the other hand, they "are" God, but seen through the veil of "Outwardness" or of "Distance".'

This chapter also confronts us with the same triad on higher planes and according to different spiritual Perspectives—Hindu, Buddhist, and Christian, as well as Islamic. 'Moreover, and even above all, Infinitude—like Perfection—is an intrinsic characteristic of the Absolute: it is as it were its inward life, or its love which, by overflowing so to speak, prolongs itself and creates the world.'

APPENDIX B

Answers to Questions About the Spiritual Master *(see p.64 note 11)*

It goes without saying that the modern seeker of a spiritual path and therefore of a Master is beset by dangers from many pseudo-esoteric groups which have nothing authentic to offer. And even an authentic spiritual order may prove not to correspond to the deepest aspirations of the seeker in question. In general it could be said that there are two kind of orders. One of these is relatively 'static', being under the direction of an authority who has not in himself any mastership beyond such guidance as he can transmit from the traditions of the order. The other is under a truly experienced guide, one who has himself spiritual realization and is capable of guiding others to it if they are sufficiently qualified.

The difference between these two orders is factual but never 'official', and the members of a 'static' order are seldom conscious of not being 'travellers'.[1] Nor must the word 'static' be taken in an absolute sense. But there are likely to be some seekers, if only a few, who are qualified for 'travel' and who, without the guidance of a veritable Master, could never do justice to their latent possibilities. What is the definition of the Master—the *guru*, the *shaykh*, the *pīr*—in the full sense of these terms?

This question is the theme of a chapter entitled 'Nature and

[1] This term is taken from Sufism.

Function of the Spiritual Master' in Schuon's *Logic and Transcendence.* Its opening passages are couched in Hindu terms,[2] but the truths it expresses are universal. The domain is in fact spiritually too central for there to be any real divergence between the different traditional forms of mysticism. All are known to insist on the three conditions mentioned here as indispensable[3] so that there is good reason to fear that if any one of the three is not fulfilled, the whole endeavour 'can only end up as a psychological exploit without any relation to the development of our higher states'. These conditions correspond to initiation, doctrine and method. The first 'results from the principle that it is impossible to approach the Absolute, or the Self, without the blessing and the aid of Heaven'. The 'blessing' in question is the sacrament of initiation which brings the recipient to a new 'birth', for the first condition of spirituality is to be virtually 'reborn'. As regards the Master, this first condition is extrinsic: unlike the others, it does not depend on his sanctity, but on his authority as duly affiliated representative of a divinely instituted mystical tradition.

The Master must also personify 'a providential doctrine', that is, a doctrine which 'depends on a Revelation in the direct and plenary sense'. The essence of the doctrine is 'truth which distinguishes between the Real and the illusory'. As an incarnation of this truth, the Master is a living presence of discernment.

Finally he must be master of 'the method which allows the initiated and consecrated contemplative to fix himself, at first mentally and later with the centre of his being, on the Real'.

It is clearly the first of these conditions which is the most frequently and easily fulfilled. The head of an authentic order which has become 'static' is necessarily qualified to bestow initiation; but only a true Master can be said to personify the doctrine

[2] This chapter was originally written for a volume presented to the Jagadguru Sri Sankarācārya Svāmigal of Kāñci Kamakoti Pitha in celebration of the fiftieth anniversary of his investiture.

[3] Apart from 'very exceptional cases' of which Schuon gives some illuminating examples.

of Ultimate Reality, and only he, as regards method, can enter into the Spiritual Path of his disciple to the point of enabling him 'to fix himself . . . on the Real'.

As to the seeker, the first condition presents no problems, since he can normally reassure himself, before taking any step, as to whether it has been fulfilled. He can also ascertain whether the order in question faithfully represents the tradition as regards both doctrine and method. But there the criteria may be said to end, if by criteria we mean what can be made the object of an investigation in the ordinary sense of the word. Yet though there is no infallible way for a would-be disciple to identify a true guide through purely mental processes, there is nonetheless a universal esoteric dictum[4] that every aspirant will find a true guide if he deserves one. It is also said that in reality and despite appearances it is not the seeker who chooses the way but the way which chooses the seeker. In other words, since the Master personifies the way, he has, mysteriously and providentially, an active function towards the seeker even before the master-disciple relationship is established by initiation. This helps to explain the following anecdote told by the Moroccan Shaykh al-'Arabī ad-Darqāwī (d. 1823), one of the very greatest masters of Sufism in recent centuries. At the moment in question he was a younger man but already a representative of his own Shaykh, 'Alī al-Jamal, to whom he complained of having to go to a place where he feared there were no spiritual people. His Shaykh cut him short with the remark: 'Beget the man you need'. And later he reiterated plurally the same command: 'Beget them!'[5] We have already seen that the initial step on the spiritual path is to be 'reborn'; and all these considerations suggest that the seeker's 'deserving' of a master must include a consciousness of 'inexistence' or emptiness, an anticipation of the

[4] See Whitall Perry, *A Treasury of Traditional Wisdom*, the section on 'the Spiritual Master', pp. 288–295, for quotations from the mystics on this point and on others related to these paragraphs.

[5] *Letters of a Sufi Master*, p. 19.

spiritual poverty (*faqr*) from which the *faqīr* takes his name. The open door is an image of this state, and the Shaykh ad-Darqāwī mentions in general that one of the most powerful means of obtaining a solution to a spiritual problem is to hold open and beware of closing 'the door of necessity'.[6] It may thus be inferred that the 'deserving' in question is to be measured by the degree of the acuteness of the seeker's sense of the necessity for a guide, and that it depends on whether his soul is sufficiently imperative, as a 'vacuum', to precipitate the advent of what he needs. Nor is such passivity incompatible with the more active attitude enjoined in Christ's 'Seek and ye shall find: knock and it shall be opened unto you', since the most powerful way of 'knocking' is prayer, and supplication is a display of emptiness and an avowal of neediness. In a word, not only the Master but also the would-be disciple has qualifications to fulfil.

[6] Ibid. p. 10.

APPENDIX C

A Question concerning the Second Vatican Council by Verax

(Published in Studies in Comparative Religion *and republished here with the author's permission.)*

There is a certain question with regard to Vatican II which, as far as we know, has not received the consideration that it deserves. There would clearly be no longer any point in examining the claims of that council's organizers and champions that it took place entirely beneath the guidance of the Holy Spirit—claims that have been reiterated[1] ad nauseam for the last twenty years. On the one hand no evidence of the Truth of this claim has ever been forthcoming; and on the other hand the lamentable results of the Council are a powerful indication that the 'Guidance' came from elsewhere. But this very fact must have prompted many to ask: 'Why was it allowed to happen?', or at least—'since evil there must be'—'Did the Holy Spirit do nothing to protect the Church? Were there no adequate signs or warning from Heaven before the disaster had taken place?' The answer to this question—or, more precisely, the answer that is offered here—begins over eighty years ago.

[1] On November 24th, 1985, at the opening of the Synod in Rome, John-Paul II gave yet another indication of his total support of Vatican II: 'At this significant moment for the life of the Church', he said, 'the Church is called to re-experience that moment of grace, the Second Vatican Council. She is called to rediscover the riches of truth contained in its documents, to mediate anew on the pastoral guidance brought to maturity then under the direction of the Spirit.'

Towards the end of the First World War, at Fatima in Portugal—it was between May and October, 1917—three shepherd children, two girls and a boy, had a series of visions of Our Lady the Blessed Virgin. She spoke only to the elder girl, Lucia, who was ten years old. The two other children, Francisco and Jacinta, nine and seven years old respectively, were brother and sister and they were Lucia's cousins. All three could see our Lady, but only the girls could hear what she said, though she told them to let Francisco share all her messages, even those which were to be kept secret for a while from everyone else. What concerns us here is the most secret message of all. But meantime, for those who are unfamiliar with the story of Fatima, there are one or two facts which need to be told, and at the risk of seeming to digress we will dwell for a moment on things which might appear to have no bearing on our initial question. Nor can we do otherwise, for the significance of what is immediately relevant here is altogether dependent on the significance of the whole.

As if by way of preparation, an Angel had appeared three times to the children in the previous year, and the third time he had given them the Blessed Sacrament. It was on May 13 of the following year that our Lady made her first appearance to them, when they were pasturing their sheep at some distance from the village where they lived. Such was her radiance that she seemed to them 'brighter than the sun', and she was more beautiful than any sight they had ever seen or imagined. She told them to come to that same place at the same hour on the thirteenth day of each of the next five months. Then she asked them if they were prepared to offer themselves to God and to bear, for the sake of others, all the sufferings that He would send them. Speaking for them all Lucia firmly assented, whereupon Our Lady told them that they would have much to suffer but that God's grace would be their strength and opening her hands she poured over them a flood of light which penetrated them through and through.

On June 13 they were not alone at the foot of the little holm oak on which Our Lady had stood. The news had spread; for although they had agreed amongst themselves to keep it a secret, Jacinta—no doubt providentially—had been unable to resist telling her family, who had told others; and if most people did not yet believe in the miraculous event, there were already some who did. That day about 50 pilgrims had come to the holy place, and the next month they were increased to nearly 3000. On October 13th, for which our Lady had told Lucia to announce a great miracle, the numbers were estimated at 100,000—men, women and children from all parts of Portugal, 'the land of Saint Mary', and beyond. As at the previous trysts, our Lady appeared only to the three little seers. No one else could see or hear her, though they could feel the blessing of her presence and see, if near enough, the rapture of those who saw. But on this occasion, after she had left them, there took place, for everyone to see, what is now known as 'the Miracle of the Sun' or 'the Dance of the Sun'. Many detailed descriptions of this phenomenon of great beauty and holiness have been recorded by eye witnesses.[2] During the miracle the Blessed Virgin appeared again to the seers, this time in the dress of Our Lady of the Rosary; then they saw the Holy Child, carried by St. Joseph who traced the Sign of the Cross over the entire gathering. That vision gave way to one of Jesus Christ in the fullness of manhood, and he likewise blessed the multitude; then they saw Our Lady of Dolours, and lastly Our Lady of Mount Carmel.

Already at the Apparition in June, Our Lady had told Lucia that she would soon take Jacinta and Francisco to Heaven, but that Lucia herself had first a mission to perform on earth, then she would follow them. Meantime she would not be left helpless and alone, for Our Lady promised never to forsake her. It was as she had said: Francisco died not quite two years after the first Apparition; his sister survived him by less than a year; Lucia, aged 94, is a nun in the Carmelite convent at Coimbra.

[2] See, for example, John de Marchi, *Fatima from the Beginning*, pp. 135–142.

More than one inspiring account has been written of the illnesses and deaths of the two younger children.[3] When Our Lady had announced their imminent departure from this world she had again opened her hands and poured light upon the three seers from the great light which surrounded her. Lucia was in that part of the light which spread over the earth, whereas the other two were in the splendour which rose to Heaven. From that time Francisco and Jacinta appeared to live only for the life to come. As to what was left of this life, it was woven, for them, of sacrifice and prayer. To read of their last months is to be conscious of a spiritual magnitude which is all the more irresistible for being in childlike mode. Retaining all the reflexes natural to their years, they displayed qualities which, while being plainly rooted in childhood, opened out onto a maturity which transcends the difference between youth and age.

On occasion they showed themselves, Lucia also, to be possessed of a remarkable heroism. In Portugal, at the time of the Apparitions, there was a powerful anti-religious movement which, politically, had gained for the moment the upper hand. The secular authorities did all they could to suppress any public manifestations of belief in the visions;[4] and one day, in an attempt to throw

[3] Ibid., pp. 169–203; see also *Fatima in Lucia's Own Words*, passim.

[4] The following extracts from a 1917 Lisbon pamphlet help to give some idea of the outlook in question: 'Citizens, as if the pernicious propaganda of reactionaries were not enough we now see a miracle trotted out in order further to degrade the people into fanaticism and superstition. There has been staged . . . an indecorous comedy in Fatima at which thousands of people have assisted, a ridiculous spectacle in which the simple people have been ingeniously deceived by means of collective suggestion . . . This, citizens, is a miserable and retrograde attempt to plunge the Portuguese people once more into the dense darkness of past times which have departed never to return The Republic and those citizens who are charged with the noble and thankless task of guiding it in the glorious paths of Civilization and Progress cannot consent to the degradation of the people into fanaticism and credulity for this would be an unpardonable failing in their primal duty not only towards their country but to Humanity as a whole. It is therefore our duty to demand from the public authorities the most energetic and immediate precautions against this shameless plan by which reaction seeks to plunge the people once more into mediaevalism . . . Citizens! Long Live the Republic! Down with reaction! Long Live Liberty!' (For the full text of this pamphlet see De Marchi, pp. 245–6.)

discredit on the whole miracle, the Mayor of Ourem kidnapped the three seers and threatened to have them boiled in oil if they would not tell him the secret which Our Lady had forbidden them to divulge. Everything was done to convince then that this was no idle threat; and they were finally taken one by one, Jacinta first, to endure, as they thought, the martyrdom of a horrible death. For each one separately, there was a final 'last chance' interrogation, but not one of them yielded; and the Mayor had to admit defeat and set them free.

Normally, when heroism was not required of them, this capacity was present as a fortitude that accompanied the other elements of which their souls seemed to be made—serenity, patience, humility, trust and magnanimity, to which must be added truth, of a scope to include not only veracity but also an implacable sense of values. These virtues were crowned by a faith which had flowered into certitude, a hope which seemed already to enjoy something of the blissful possession of its object, and a whole-hearted love for the Divine, which was totally free from any reserve.

Francisco was buried in the little cemetery at Fatima. But Jacinta was not destined to end her days at home: the doctors insisted on transferring her to a hospital in Lisbon, where she died after an operation. Her body was placed in the Church of the Holy Angels where for three days it was visited by the faithful and continued to give the impression of sleep rather than death. Many bore witness to the wonderful scent which filled the room above the sacristy where it was laid. When the coffin had been sealed, it was taken to a vault in Villa Nova de Ourem. She had said however that after her death she would return to Fatima.

It was only in 1930 that the Church's long reserve of judgement came to a conclusion. The visions were formally declared to be worthy of belief and the cult of Our Lady of Fatima was officially allowed. Five years later the Bishop of Leiria decided that the body of Jacinta should be moved to Fatima and buried there beside her brother in a new tomb which had been built for them both. For some reason, before the coffin was moved to its final destination, it was opened; and it was then seen that death had had no power to corrupt the body of Jacinta, whose face was still as it had been fifteen years previously when she was lying in state in the Church of the Holy Angels.

Throughout the six months of the Apparitions, the messages which Lucia was told to make public, at that time or later, were largely concerned with the need to propagate devotion to the Rosary and devotion to our Lady's Immaculate Heart. They were also largely concerned with the general need for mankind to change the direction in which it was now moving. Failure to make that change would bring down the most terrible punishments; and for a beginning, although the present war would soon end, a worse war would follow it. As an unmistakable sign of its imminence when the time was not far off, the night sky would be lit by a great light which would have no apparent cause and which would last long enough for millions of people to take note of it. The light duly appeared an hour or two before midnight on January 24th 1938, and it was seen all over Europe causing a considerable albeit soon forgotten sensation.

The most secret of the messages was eventually written down by Lucia and placed in an envelope which she then sealed, with instructions that it must not be opened until 1960. It was kept for many years in the palace of the Bishop of Leiria. Then it was transferred to the Vatican, where it has remained ever since in the pontifical apartments.

The years passed, and in 1957, under the auspices of Pope Pius XII, the process of beatification of Francisco and Jacinta was instituted. This meant that a prominent member of the commission concerned with the process had to make an official visit to Sister Lucia to interrogate her about the last days of her two fellow seers; and amongst what was published later, apart from what concerned the immediate purpose of the interview, there were certain general remarks made by Sister Lucia of which we may quote the following: 'Three times Our Lady has told me that we are approaching the latter days . . . The Lord will punish the world very soon . . . Many nations will vanish from the face of the earth.'

The Pope died in the following year. Two years later his successor, in the presence of Cardinals Ottaviani and Bacci, duly opened the envelope which contained the secret. He may have shown it to them, and perhaps to others also; but instead of giving its message to the world, as had been expected, he made no public comment, nor has the Vatican ever broken this silence. But in October 1963 an article headed 'The Future of Mankind' was published in Stuttgart[5] purporting to give the gist of the message of Fatima. There was nothing to guarantee that the contents of the article were in fact a summary of the contents of the long-sealed envelope; yet although the publication was brought to the notice of the Vatican, whose custom it is to deny false rumours immediately, no official comment whatsoever was forthcoming. In Portugal itself the Archbishop of Oviedo was reported by the press as having said that he presumed the Portuguese episcopacy would make an official pronouncement on the subject; but nothing of the kind ever took place; and rightly or wrongly, this total silence on the part of all the church authorities, both the greater and the lesser, was interpreted by priest and layman as a confirmation of the authenticity of the text in question. It was translated into Portuguese and also into Spanish, and was published throughout the Iberian Peninsula and elsewhere. The essence of it lies in what are almost its opening words: 'A punishment will befall the entire human race.' We must add also the following quotation which would explain, if the document is indeed the long awaited Fatima message, why the Vatican should have been unwilling to make it public: 'The human race has sinned and trampled beneath its feet the gift that was bestowed upon it. Nowhere does order reign. Satan has reached the very highest places and decides the march of

[5] *Neu-Europa*, 15. x. 63.

events. He will succeed in insinuating himself into the Church and in reaching its highest summit.'

From the modernist standpoint, what could have been less opportune? Roncalli had recalled Montini from Milan to the Vatican and made him a cardinal. Together they and others were planning the Council,[6] which was to reform the Church most drastically in what Montini later described as 'the intention of making Christianity acceptable and lovable, indulgent and open, free from mediaeval rigorism and from taking a pessimistic view of man and his customs,'[7] and now, just at this moment of would-be euphory, the Pope was called upon to make public, in the name of Our Lady, a message altogether in line with 'mediaeval rigorism'. In a word, he was being asked by Heaven to discredit the Council in advance, by warning the faithful to be on their guard against Satanic initiatives and manoeuvres, a warning which would inevitably have the effect of prejudicing them and making them suspicious of all new departures in pastoral directives. The purpose of the Council was to open the door to change; and Roncalli well knew that the Church was millennially prone to dismiss all innovations as the work of the devil. His predecessor, Pius XII, had said: 'One must condemn anything that seems animated by the unhealthy spirit of novelty; anything . . . that suggests new orientations for the Christian life; anything that suggests new directions for the Church to follow or new hopes and aspirations that are more suitable to the souls of modern day Catholics.'[8]

But if the new Pope chose to remain silent about the contents of the envelope, it must be remembered that there were still at that time some highly placed Vatican officials who were of one mind with Pope Pius XII, in particular Cardinal Ottaviani; and by 1963, with the election of Montini as Paul VI, the dangers of

[6] See, in this connection, Rama Coomaraswamy. *The Destruction of the Christian Tradition*, pp. 88–91.

[7] Doc. Cath. No. 1538.

[8] *Pleni 'Animo.*

modernism were clearer than they had been in 1960. It was therefore all the more imperative that the message of Our Lady should no longer be withheld—whence no doubt the decision, by a traditionalist with access to the document, that since he could not disclose it officially, he would find some unofficial means of bringing at least the gist of it to the attention of the public.

It was scarcely to be expected however that Heaven would rest content with such a clandestine transmission of a mere summary of its message. Nor in fact do we need to dwell on that text, despite the near certainty of its genuineness; for as soon as it became clear that the Church did not intend to reveal the secret of Fatima, over two years before the Stuttgart publication, another message was already on its way to mankind.

On the North coast of Spain, all along the southern shores of the Bay of Biscay, the land rises up steeply from the sea; and less than fifty miles inland, South West of the coastal town of Santander, there is a small mountain village named San Sebastian de Garabandal, relatively untouched by the modern world, a cluster of houses together with a church and a school, some seventy homes in all. It was on a Sunday afternoon, not far from Midsummer's Day, in the June of 1961. Three twelve year old girls and a fourth girl of eleven had decided to steal a few apples from the schoolmaster's tree. This they did, but when they had eaten their fill, their consciences began to trouble them. Only the other day the parish priest had told them that whenever they did anything wrong the devil rejoiced but their guardian Angels were sadly grieved. They were now outside the village in a sunken lane which led up to a group of pines. It was strewn with stones of all shapes and sizes, many of them rough and sharp. Conchita, the leader of the escapade, proposed that they should throw some of these at the devil as a punishment for having tempted them, and the others at once agreed. Each one of them was sincerely distressed by thoughts of the sorrow of the Angels in Heaven; and having decided that the devil was situated at a certain spot to their left, they set about stoning him with all their strength. This vigorous and wholehearted rite of repentance brought relief to their troubled consciences; and when they felt they had thrown enough stones, they gathered some of the smaller rounded pebbles and sat down to play at marbles.

All of a sudden three of the girls, Mary Loly, Jacinta and Maria Cruz, were conscious that their leader was no longer with them in the game. The colour had ebbed from Conchita's cheeks, and she was staring straight in front of her with a rapt expression on her face. They thought she must be ill, and Mary Loly jumped to her feet to run for help, but Conchita made a gesture of pointing with her clasped hands, and said: 'Look!' They all turned from her to see what she was looking at, and when they saw they too were rapt. There, in front of them, was an Angel, surrounded by a light which for all its brightness did not dazzle them. He had wings such as they had seen in icons of the Annunciation, and he was near enough for them to notice that the blue robe he was wearing had no seams in it. Although he looked only about nine years old, a boy of amazing beauty, he gave the impression of great strength. Then he vanished.

Overwhelmed with awe, the girls ran back to the village. On the way they were stopped by another girl who was struck by the pallor of their faces and asked them what was the matter. They said they had seen an Angel, and the girl repeated this to many others. The first thought of the visionaries was to go to the church, but once there they were afraid to enter it. In tears they went round to the back of the building, and there they sat and sobbed. It was not long before they were noticed by some smaller children who asked them why they were weeping. Again they said it was because they had seen an Angel, whereupon the children ran to tell the schoolmistress. It was not long before the four girls summoned up courage enough to enter the church, and they were still there when the schoolmistress arrived. Their answers to her questions convinced her that they were speaking the truth, and before they left for their different homes she led them in a Rosary of thanksgiving.

By next morning there was scarcely a soul in the village who had not heard the news. Soon after midday the parish priest arrived from Cosio and questioned the girls one by one. He too was inclined to believe them, and he told Conchita that if they saw the Angel again, they should ask him who he was and why he had come. As to the villagers, a few believed at once, but others were frankly sceptical, while the majority preferred to wait and see. The next evening the girls went again to the sunken lane, and kneeling at the place where they had seen the Angel they recited the Rosary. But this time they saw nothing, and at nightfall they returned to the village amid the jeers of some who had followed them. Before going to bed however all four girls, each in her respective home, heard a voice say: 'Do not be troubled; you will see me again.'

The next evening they went once again to their place of vision. This time they were alone. Again the Angel did not appear, but as they made their way back to the village the light which had surrounded him suddenly blocked their path. It soon faded, but something of its glow remained in their souls. The next day they had the idea that they should invite an older person to accompany them to their tryst in the sunken lane, and others joined them on the way, so that several adults were present to take part in the Rosary. After the second decade the four girls suddenly became rapt. Their faces, pale and luminous, seemed to reflect a light; and they were all gazing slightly upwards at something well above the level of the lane where they were kneeling. For the second time the Angel had come. He stood in the air, as if supported by his surrounding light. 'Who are you?', said one of the girls. 'Why have you come?' But he did not answer. The men and women could see nothing of him or of his light, but they could plainly see the girls' reactions and that was enough to convince them all that these children had truly been blessed with a vision.

The news now spread to the surrounding hamlets, and every

afternoon visitors climbed up the steep path to Garabandal to witness—as they hoped—the sight of the girls in ecstasy and to feel, if only at second hand, something of their intense happiness which was too radiant not to communicate itself to others. But some days there was no vision, and the visitors returned in disappointment.

On Saturday July 1st there was a larger gathering than ever before. Some of those present had come from more distant parts of Spain, and there were a number of priests as well as doctors and journalists. On this occasion the vision lasted for two hours, and for the first time the Angel spoke. He told them that he was Michael, and it was conveyed to their understanding that he was St. Michael the Archangel. He also said that the next day the Blessed Virgin would come to them, and that he would be with her.

The following afternoon it was Sunday—crowds of visitors walked up to Garabandal, and at about six o'clock the girls set off for the lane, followed by a multitude. A rough square enclosure had been made at the place of the Archangel's first appearance to separate and protect the visionaries from the dense throngs of well meaning albeit often inconsiderate spectators. But before they had reached this point they were suddenly in the presence of Our Lady of Mount Carmel, for so it was that she appeared to them. They said afterwards that she seemed to be about seventeen years old and that she was clad in a white robe with a blue mantle. On her head was a golden crown which they described as 'a crown of stars'. They had never seen such beauty of face or heard such beauty of voice. St. Michael stood on one side of her, and on the other side was a similar celestial being who might have been his twin brother.

Only Conchita and her three friends could see the vision, and they alone could hear what Our Lady said. From that day, July 2nd 1961, she made herself present to the four girls in a series of Apparitions which continued over a period of more than four years, frequent at first, but less so from January 1963. Her final appearance, which she said would be the last, was to Conchita alone on November 13th, 1965.

It was impossible for those who witnessed the visitations—especially for those who did so regularly—not to believe that here was a Divine intervention. The girls always knew when and where a vision was to take place, wherever they might be. Each received three inner calls, and at the third call they would all run simultaneously, sometimes from opposite directions, to the same place. As soon as Our Lady appeared, they would be as it were withdrawn from the earthly plane, aware of each other, but totally unaware of the onlookers, who were unable to cause them physical sensations. People even stuck pins into them to see if they would react, which they did not, and lights were flashed close to their eyes which never even blinked, though as soon as the vision had gone they would complain of the brightness of the photographers' lights with which they were beset on all sides. Another significant fact was the great weight which their bodies would acquire: it took two strong men to lift one of them when she was contemplating Our Lady or St. Michael, but at such times the visionaries could lift each other with far greater ease than normally. The astonished spectators would see one of them lift another high into the air as if she were a doll so that she could hand the Blessed Virgin a rosary to kiss or some other object to bless. Sometimes St. Michael appeared alone, as at first, and Our Lady sometimes appeared with him and his brother, sometimes alone, and sometimes carrying the child Jesus in her arms. Once or twice she gave him to the girls to hold, and they were seen to make all the gestures of cradling a babe in arms. They said that he had no weight, nor could they feel the touch of him, but he none the less occupied a space in the sense that when their hands reached him they could go no further.

The full story of these miraculous events has been chronicled elsewhere,[9] nor would it be relevant to recount it here in any further detail. What concerns us is what Our Lady said to the children and in particular to Conchita. Nor must we forget that the

[9] F. Sanchez-Ventura y Pascual, *The Apparitions of Garabandal* (San Miguel Publishing Company, Detroit).

messages of Garabandal coincided exactly with the preparations for the Second Vatican Council and with the actual Council itself.

'"The Cup"[10] was already filling; it is now full to overflowing. Many cardinals, many bishops and many priests are on the road to perdition, and with them they are taking many more souls.'[11] This is part of one of the final messages of Garabandal. The children had already been shown the terrible punishment[12] which threatens mankind as a result of the present trend of humanity. It is instructive to consider, against the background of these messages, the precipitate eagerness of the Council to pander to this trend, an eagerness personified by Paul VI, and overflowing from his words: 'We moderns, men of our own day, wish everything to be new. Our old people, the Traditionalists the Conservatives, measured the value of things according to their enduring quality. We instead, are actualists, we want everything to be new all the time, to be expressed in a continually improvised and dynamically unusual form.'[13] The same speaker defined his 'Post-conciliar Church' by saying that it 'seeks to adapt itself to the languages, to the customs and to the inclinations of the men of our times, men completely engrossed in the rapidity of material evolution.'[14] He also said:

[10] It was already clear from previous messages that 'the Cup' meant the Cup of Divine Anger.

[11] See in connection with this particular message, Fr. Joseph A. Pelletier, *God Speaks at Garabandal* (Assumption Publications. Worcester, Mass.) p.44.

[12] Unlike the messages of Fatima, those of Garabandal included the prophecy of a warning and a miracle which would precede the punishment. The warning, so it was said, would be seen throughout the whole world as a sign which could have no natural cause. It would bring many people of all religions to a consciousness of guilt, and many unbelievers would believe. The visionaries were told what it would be, but not when. As to the miracle, it would only be witnessed in the region of Garabandal; but Conchita was ordered to announce it eight days in advance, so that all who wished to see it might have time to assemble. It would be more overwhelming than the miracle of Fatima and would be accompanied by many lesser miracles—miraculous cures of the sick—and by many conversions. When it had been fulfilled, a sign of it would be left at the cluster of pines outside the village, and that sign would remain until the end of the world.

[13] See Rama Coomaraswamy, ibid. p.92.

[14] Ibid., p.132.

'From the start the Council has propagated a wave of serenity and optimism, a Christianity that is exciting and positive, loving life, mankind and earthly values.'[15]

There was yet another very clear indication of the attitude of Heaven towards Vatican II. To this particular sign, altogether striking enough in itself, even further attention was unwittingly and most ironically drawn by John-Paul II in one of his attempts to demonstrate that the Divine Blessing had been on the Council. He describes Montini as 'the Pope of that deep change which was nothing but a revelation of the face of the Church, awaited by the man and the world of today'. He also said: 'John XXIII and after him, Paul VI, received from the Holy Spirit the charisma of transformation'; and he would have us take Montini's death on the feast of the Transfiguration as a proof of God's presence and activity at another remarkable change, namely the 'transformation' of the Church subsequent to Vatican II: 'The Lord, having called Pope Paul to Himself on the solemnity of this feast of the Transfiguration, permitted him and us to know that in the whole work of transformation, of renewal of the Church in the Spirit of Vatican II, He is present as He was in the marvellous event which took place on Mount Tabor.'[16] The mystery of the Transfiguration on the one hand; the trivialization of the sacraments and the liturgy on the other. It would be difficult to find a more incongruous parallel.

The effrontery of likening the changes made by Montini to the event on Mount Tabor is all the greater because there was in fact, at his death, a manifest alert to the contrary, an occurrence which was the exact opposite of the Transfiguration, as if the Feast had wished to disown the person whose death had coincided with it, and as if Providence had wished to make manifest Its condemnation of the man and his works. It must not be forgotten that ever since the Council of Trent anathemas have been regularly invoked upon anyone who should alter the Tridentine Mass; and to what Paul VI

[15] Doc. Cath. No.1538.

[16] See Rama Coomaraswamy, ibid., p.102.

earned from the past, there must be added the terrible curse which he called down upon his own head when he took the papal oath before his enthronement, swearing on pain of damnation to make no changes and to allow none to be made in the traditions of the Church, but to safeguard what he had received. At death, to the great embarrassment of those who had to organize the lying-in-state, the body of this heavily laden soul began to decompose with an altogether abnormal rapidity. No amount of incense seemed to be enough; and the stench of the corpse was matched by its appearance.[17] Considering the nature of the occasion, it is impossible to maintain that this was not a sign from Heaven.

[17] For an account by an eye-witness, see Peter Hebblethwaite, *The Year of the Three Popes*, p.6.

APPENDIX D

St. Malachy's Prophecy of the Popes[1]

St. Malachy O'Morgair was born in Armagh in Ireland about 1094. At a remarkably early age he became Bishop of Connor, and then Archbishop of Armagh. In 1139, on his way to Rome, he stopped at the Abbey of Clairvaux where he became so attached to St. Bernard that on reaching his destination he begged the Pope to allow him to end his days in spiritual retreat amongst the holy abbot's disciples. The Pope not merely refused to allow this, but even added to St. Malachy's administrative responsibilities by making him Papal Legate for Ireland. But in a sense the Irish Saint had his wish. He was in continual correspondence with St. Bernard, and with his collaboration he founded, in 1142, the first Cistercian monastery in Ireland. Six years later he set out on a second visit to Rome and stopped again at Clairvaux, where he was taken seriously ill; and it was actually in the arms of St. Bernard himself that he died some three weeks later, having told the monks that his illness would be fatal. St. Bernard preached a most eloquent sermon at the funeral; and so great was his esteem and affection for St. Malachy that he dedicated another sermon to him a year later, on the anniversary of his death, and also wrote a short biography of him for the edification of the faithful.

St. Malachy was canonized by Pope Clement III in 1190, and the

[1] This article was first published in *Tomorrow*, Summer 1966 and then again, on request, in *Studies in Comparative Religion*, Vol. 16, nos. 2 and 3. We publish it here because the prophecy itself was clearly made more for the people of the eleventh hour than for St. Malachy's own contemporaries.

celebration of his feast is on November 3rd, the day after his death. His life was remarkably rich in miracles and visions;[2] but neither in St. Bernard's biography nor in other contemporary sources is there any mention of a prophecy about the Popes. This has always been the chief argument of those who have doubted its authenticity. None the less, suffice it to say here that if the prophecy in question is a mere invention, then clearly it was not St. Malachy who invented it. But if it is a genuine prophecy—and this article may help the reader to make up his mind on that score—then it is more reasonable to assume that St. Malachy himself was the author, as tradition tells us, than to suppose that it should be rightfully ascribed to some other person who was endowed with the gifts of the Spirit.

Moreover, if St. Bernard did not single it out for mention, or even if he knew nothing about it, there is an obvious explanation. St. Malachy was a man of so many undoubted miracles, and so many visions which had proved true in his life-time, that by comparison the prophecy of the Popes was not worth mentioning. Its truth had yet to be proved. In itself, at that time, it could not have seemed to be of any particular significance. Who would have been interested to hear that there would be 112 more Popes between then and Doomsday? It would have seemed incredible to almost everyone that the second coming of Christ could be so far off. Nor is the text of the prophecy in any way sensational. Only one Pope is actually mentioned by name and, as for the others, each is indicated by no more than a short Latin phrase which often refers to nothing of greater interest than the family coat of arms of the man in question.

[2] As St. Bernard tells us. St. Malachy had been questioned some years previously by his disciples at Melfont Abbey as to where of all places he would wish to die and be buried. He had replied that if it were to be in Ireland, he would wish it to be beside the tomb of St. Patrick. but that otherwise he would wish it to be at the Abbey of Clairvaux. They then asked him what day of all days in the year he would choose for his death and he replied that he would choose the Feast of All Souls. (See Ailbe J. Luddy, *Life of St. Malachy*, M.H. Gill and Son, Dublin, 1950.)

Presumably, since the prophecy refers to the future, its vision and formulation took place during the reign of Pope Innocent II who died in 1143. At any rate, the first Pope mentioned in the text is indicated by the words *Excastro Tiberis*, 'from a castle on the Tiber,' and this clearly refers to Pope Innocent's successor, Celestine II, who was born in a castle near the town of Castello on the River Tiber. That the opening of the prophecy refers to this Pope is made doubly clear by the fact that the second reign is summed up in the words *Inimicus expulsus*, 'the enemy driven out,' and Celestine II 's successor, Lucius II, who reigned for only a few months (1144–1145), had the family name of *Caccianemici*, which expresses precisely the idea of driving out enemies.

To take another early example, Nicholas Breakspeare, the only Englishman ever to become Pope—he was Pope Adrian IV (1154–1159)—is designated by the words *De rure albo* which mean literally 'from out of the white country' or more precisely 'countryside'. The 'white country' is Albion, so called because it appears 'white' to those who come to it by the nearest possible sea route. But the adjective *albus* has repercussions which go beyond the name of Albion in this context, for although Nicholas Breakspeare was of 'rural' origin, he may be considered also as a man of St. Albans which was the nearest town to his native village; and at the time when he was elected Pope he was Cardinal Bishop of Albano in Italy.

The prophecy did not become generally known until the end of the sixteenth century, more than 400 years after St. Malachy's death. It was at Venice, in 1595, that Arnold Wion published his *Lignum Vitae* (The Tree of Life), a collection of short biographies of eminent members of the Benedictine Order in its many branches, of which the Cistercian Order is one; and in connection with St. Malachy the text of the prophecy was included. It immediately caused a stir, but some had doubts about its authenticity. Such doubts were grounded not only on the absence of any extrinsic or intrinsic evidence that it was the work of St. Malachy, but also on the fact that the antipopes were included in the list as well as the true Popes whose function they had usurped. It must be admitted however, that the inclusion of the antipopes can also be taken as an argument on the other side, since it is scarcely conceivable that a midsixteenth-century forger would have deliberately 'marred' his fabrication by including anyone who was not a true Pope. On the other hand, assuming that this is not a forgery, it is by no means the only true prophecy, to say the least, which contains certain 'stumbling blocks'. What is puzzling is not so much that the text should include the antipopes as that it should condemn only two of them outright (which it does by applying to them the words *schismaticus* and *schisma*), while speaking of the others in apparently 'neutral' terms. Whatever the explanation may be—and it is unlikely to be forthcoming, for presumably we shall never know the form of the vision on which the prophecy was based—those who denied outright its authenticity at the time of its publication, or soon after, appear to have been comparatively few. It was accepted as genuine by many, even in some Protestant circles. Others not unnaturally preferred to reserve their judgement. As far as the past was concerned, the truth of the text was crystal clear; but it is easy to forge a 'true prophecy' about the past. If, however, this was not a forgery, the future could be relied on to demonstrate its truth.

Today, now that more than another 400 years have gone by, most of that future has become past history, and the prophecy has certainly stood the test of time. As regards the text itself, it is not possible to make a distinction between that part of it which was already past at the date of publication and what was still in the future. Its brief descriptions continue to be so apt that confirmed sceptics have been driven to wonder whether the Cardinals did not sometimes choose a Pope to fit the prophecy, or in other cases whether the Pope himself had not deliberately taken action to make the prophecy 'come true'. Would Pope Pius VI (1775–1799) have taken the then altogether unprecedented step of paying a visit to the imperial court of Vienna if he had not been styled

Peregrinus Apostolicus, 'the journeying heir of the Apostles'? But there were, in fact, compelling political reasons for that initiative; nor in any case would a single state visit to a neighbouring country be adequate to the word peregrinus which suggests more in the way of travel. That 'more' was to come: the prophecy not seldom refers to unforeseeable things over which neither Pope nor Cardinals could have the slightest control, and the papacy of Pius VI is a case in point for the word *peregrinus* would seem to refer above all to the tragic end of his life, which he certainly had not planned. In 1798 he was taken prisoner by the French Republican army and forced to travel from Rome to Siena, then to Florence, then Turin, from there across the Alps to Briançon, then to Embrun, Gap, Grenoble, and finally Valence where only death put an end to his 'peregrinations', for the Directoire had already decided to transfer him to Dijon. But if all this was tragic from an individual point of view it was also, to the exasperation of his atheist captors, something of a triumphal procession—such were the marks of devotion shown to the Pope by the people of Italy and France wherever he went.

Another feature of the prophecy which rules out any planning ahead is that the text does not always refer directly to the Pope himself, so that even after the election it may continue to be a riddle, which is however always solved before the death of the pontiff in question. Pius VI was succeeded by Pius VII (1800–1823) whose reign is indicated by the words *Aquila rapax*, 'the rapacious eagle'. These words could not possibly be made to fit the newly elected Pope; but after nine years it suddenly became clear that the *aquila* was Napoleon, who is often described as eagle-like in appearance and who proved himself 'rapacious' by snatching the Pope from Rome and keeping him captive at Savona from 1809 and then at Fontainbleau from 1812 until his own fortunes began to decline and Pius was eventually able to return to Rome where he showed himself extremely magnanimous both to the exiled and dying emperor and to the Bonaparte family in general.

Another striking designation is *De Balneis Etruriae*, 'from the baths of Etruria,' which refers to Pope Gregory XVI (1831–1846) who was of the Order of the Camaldoli, which originated at Balneo (from the Latin *balneum* which means bath) in Tuscany, as Etruria is now called. Passing on from him, the papacy of Pius IX (1846–78) is referred to in the words *Crux de cruce*, 'cross from cross,' generally taken to mean that the troubles of this Pope, the cross he had to bear, came to him from the House of Savoy, whose coat of arms has a cross as its most dominant feature. These troubles culminated in the capture of Rome by King Victor Emmanuel in 1870 and the Pope's loss of what little temporal power he had left.

The next Pope, Leo XIII (1878–1903), is *Lumen in caelo*, 'a light in heaven'; and whatever more profound meaning this may have also, it is sufficiently explained by the arms of the Pecci family in which there is a comet on an azure ground. Much the same may be said of his successor, Pius X (1903–1914) whose reign is indicated by the device *Ignis ardens*, 'a blazing fire', which finds an immediate explanation in the six-rayed star that figures in his family arms. During his reign those who knew the prophecy were in some trepidation with regard to the words *Religio depopulata*, 'the depopulated religion,' which denoted the reign of the Pope who was to follow. It was predicted that during the reign of this Pope atheism would take thousands of men and women away from religion. This in fact happened; and although the spread of atheism had started before and has been continuing ever since, it was actually in this reign that the first communist state was established. That key to the prophecy was not available until three years after the election. But it was not necessary to wait until then to see the aptitude of St. Malachy's words. By the time that the Pope in question, Benedict XV, came to the throne, in the autumn of 1914, another tragic cause of 'depopulation'—but in a totally different sense—had become only too clear.

The next device, *Fides intrepida*, 'intrepid faith,' is less striking but it is none the less particularly apt with regard to Achille Ratti, Pope Pius XI. As to the next, St. Malachy here leans as it were across a span of 800 years to pay tribute to one of the most saintly of the Popes, for Pius XII (1939–1958) is *Pastor angelicus*, 'the angelic shepherd'.

Many will remember that in his reign the words *Pastor et nauta* 'shepherd and sailor', which denotes his successor, were often interpreted to mean that a non-Italian would be elected, one who would have to come to the Vatican from across the sea. Might it not be Cardinal Spellman for example? But it had escaped people's notice that one of Italy's Cardinals was already in any case a sailor, whether he had to cross the sea to the Vatican or not, and that was the Patriarch of Venice, for every Venetian, that is, everyone whose normal means of transport is the gondola, may be called *nauta*. Moreover Roncalli (John XXIII) had also been, in his youth, a shepherd in the literal sense.

Flos florum, 'the flower of flowers', that is, the lily, comes next in the prophecy, and as in the case of *Lumen in caelo* the meaning is clearly heraldic, for the fleur-de-lis is a prominent feature of the arms of the Montinis, the family of Paul VI. As to the words *De medietate lunae*, 'concerning the middle (or the half) of the moon' which denote the reign of his successor, they had been, over the centuries, the basis of some strange speculations. In general it was concluded that since the half moon had no particular significance it must be the crescent that was indicated, and that the reference was therefore to Islam. Some even predicted that under this pontiff there would be general conversion of Muslims to Christianity. No one thought that 'the moon' could simply mean 'the month'. If that suggestion had been made, it would have been dismissed as pointless by the question: 'What month?'. The true answer, 'the single month for which he will reign', could only have been given by St. Malachy himself, or one like him. The reference is clearly to the inauspicious sign which was to be seen exactly at the middle of the lunar month when the rising full moon was eclipsed; and we are now in a pontificate which is expressly related to an eclipse, *De labore solis*, 'concerning the eclipse of the sun', yet another of those devices which will only become clear in due course.

At this point a few observations may not be out of place, if only for the sake of those who, without time for reflection, are here newly confronted with this laconic list of Popes, which might well give rise to mixed feelings. The devices are apt enough; but to what purpose was the prophecy made? The motive behind it seems to have been exclusively quantitative, that of a chronicler bent on registering carefully, with no omissions, everyone who could be said from any point of view to have held a papal office, even the antipopes. We look in vain for any qualitative element whatsoever, apart from the praise implicit in the devices which denote the last two Piuses, *Fides intrepida* and *Pastor angelicus*. But a moment's reflection tells us that this document has indeed the right to be purely quantitative, and that therein, precisely, lies its purpose. We realise moreover that in it St. Malachy is speaking, not to the men of his own times, but directly to us and through us to all men now alive; for if it is of little interest to be told that there will be a hundred and twelve more Popes, it is quite another matter to be told that there will only be two more, and that is what the prophecy tells us today. These last two pontificates are denoted as follows:

111 *De gloria olivae*, 'concerning the glory of the olive.'

112 *In persecutione extrema sacrae Romanae Ecclesiae sedebit Petrus Romanus qui pascet oves in multis tribulationibus; quibis transactis civitas septicollis diruetur, et Judex tremendus judicabit populum*, 'In the final persecution of the Holy Roman Church, Roman Peter will sit upon the throne. He will feed his flock amid many tribulations, and when these things have been brought to pass, the city of the seven hills will be destroyed and the terrible Judge will judge the people.'

Bibliography

BLACK ELK:

see Brown, Joseph Epes and Neihardt, John G.

BROWN, JOSEPH EPES:

The Sacred Pipe (Black Elk's Account of the Seven Rites of the Oglala Sioux), University of Oklahoma Press, 1989.

BURCKHARDT, TITUS:

An Introduction to Sufi Doctrine, Thorsons, 1976.
Sacred Art in East and West, Fons Vitae, 2001.
Siena, City of the Virgin, Oxford University Press, 1958.
Moorish Culture in Spain, Fons Vitae, 1999.
Alchemy: Science of the Cosmos, Science of the Soul, Fons Vitae, 1997.
Art of Islam, World of Islam Festival Trust, 1976.
Mystical Astrology according to Ibn Arabi, Beshara Publications, 1989.
Fez, City of Islam, The Islamic Texts Society, 1992.
Mirror of the Intellect, Quinta Essentia, 1987.
Chartres and the Birth of the Cathedral, Golgonooza Press, 1995.

CHITTICK, WILLIAM C:

The Sufi Doctrine of Rumi (*An Introduction*), Tehran, 1974.

The Sufi Path of Love (*The Spiritual Teachings of Rumi*), State University of New York Press, 1983.
The Sufi Path of Knowledge: Ibn al-'Arabi's Metaphysics of Imagination, State University of New York Press, 1989.
Faith and Practice of Islam, State University of New York Press, 1992.
Imaginal Worlds: Ibn al-'Arabi and the Problem of Religious Diversity, State University of New York Press, 1994.
Sufism (*A Short Introduction*), One World, 2000.

CLARK, ROBERT E D:
Darwin: Before and After (An Examination and an Assessment), Paternoster Press, 1958.

COOMARASWAMY, ANANDA K:
Coomaraswamy: Selected Papers, vol. 1: Traditional Art and Symbolism, vol.2: Metaphysics, vol.3: *Coomaraswamy: His Life and Work* (by Roger Lipsey), Princeton University Press, 1977.
Christian and Oriental Philosophy of Art, Dover Publications, 1956.
The Transformation of Nature in Art, Dover Publications, 1956.
The Mirror of Gesture, Dover Publications, 1958.
The Dance of Shiva, Dover Publications, 1985.
The Bugbear of Literacy, Sophia Perennis, 1979.
What is Civilization? And Other Essays, Golgonooza Press, 1989.

COOMARASWAMY, RAMA P:
The Destruction of the Christian Tradition, Sophia Perennis, 1981.

AD-DARQĀWĪ, AL-ʿARABĪ:

Letters of a Sufi Master, the Shaikh al-ʿArabī ad-Darqāwī (translated by Titus Burckhardt), Fons Vitae, 1998.

DENTON, MICHAEL:

Evolution: A Theory in Crisis, Burnett Books, 1985.

DEWAR, DOUGLAS:

The Transformist Illusion, Sophia Perennis, 1995.

EATON, GAI:

King of the Castle (*Choice and Responsibility in the Modern World*), The Islamic Texts Society, 1990.
Islam and the Destiny of Man, The Islamic Texts Society, 1994.
Remembering God: Reflections on Islam, The Islamic Texts Society, 2001.

FERNANDO, RANJIT:

The Unanimous Tradition, Essays on the Essential Unity of all religions. Edited by Ranjit Fernando, Sri Lanka Institute of Traditional Studies, 1991.

GUÉNON, RENÉ:

Introduction to the Study of the Hindu Doctrines, Sophia Perennis, 1998.
Man and His Becoming according to the Vedânta, Sophia Perennis, 2000.
The Crisis of the Modern World, Sophia Perennis, 1996.
The Reign of Quantity and the Signs of the Times, Sophia Perennis, 1995.
The Symbolism of the Cross, Sophia Perennis, 1995.

The Multiple States of Being, Sophia Perennis, 2001.
The Fallacy of Spiritualism, Sophia Perennis, 2002.
The Great Triad, Quinta Essentia, 1991.
Fundamental Symbols, The Universal Language of Sacred Science, Quinta Essentia, 1995.

HÔNEN:

Hônen the Buddhist Saint, by Shunjô (translated and edited by Harper Havelock Coates and Ryugaku Ishizuka), Kyoto, 1949.

IBN 'ARABĪ, MUḤYI'D-DĪN:

Wisdom of the Prophets, Extracts from Fuṣūṣ al-Ḥikam (translated and annotated by Titus Burckhardt), Beshara Publications, 1975.
The Bezels of Wisdom, Fuṣūṣ al-Ḥikam (translated by R. W. J. Austin), Paulist Press, 1980.
Tarjumān al-Ashwāq (A Collection of Mystical Odes, edited and translated by R. A. Nicholson), Theosophical Publishing House, 1978.
Sufis of Andalusia; The Rūh al-Quds and ad-Durrat al-Fākhirah (translated and annotated by R. W. J. Austin), Beshara Publications, 1988.

IBN 'ATĀ'ILLĀH, AHMAD:

Sufi Aphorisms, Kitab al-Ḥikam (translated with an introduction and notes by Victor Danner), E. J. Brill, 1973.

AL-JĪLĪ, 'ABD AL-KARĪM:

Universal Man, Extracts from al-Insān al-Kāmil (translated and annotated by Titus Burckhardt), Beshara Publications, 1995.

KEEBLE, BRIAN:

Art: For Whom and For What?, Golgonooza Press, 1998.

LINDBOM, TAGE:

The Tares and the Good Grain, Mercer University Press, 1984.

LINGS, MARTIN:

A Sufi Saint of the Twentieth Century: Shaykh Aḥmad al-'Alawī, The Islamic Texts Society, 1993.
The Quranic Art of Calligraphy and Illumination, World of Islam Festival Trust, 1977.
Ancient Beliefs and Modern Superstitions, Archetype, 2001.
What is Sufism? The Islamic Texts Society, 1995.
Muhammad: His Life Based on the Earliest Sources, The Islamic Texts Society, 1998.
The Sacred Art of Shakespeare, (*To Take upon Us the Mystery of Things*), Inner Traditions International, 1998.
Collected Poems, (second edition augmented), Archetype, 2002.
The Book of Certainty (*The Sufi Doctrine of Faith, Vision and Gnosis*), The Islamic Texts Society, 1992.
Symbol & Archetype, (*A Study of the Meaning of Existence*), Quinta Essentia, 1997.
The Eleventh Hour, Archetype, 2002.
Mecca, Archetype, 2002.
Summits of Qur'an Calligraphy and Illumination, Thesaurus Islamicus Foundation, forthcoming.

LIPSEY, ROGER:
Coomaraswamy: His Life and Work (vol. 3 of *Coomaraswamy: Selected Papers*, see Coomaraswamy, A. K.), Princeton University Press, 1977.

LUCIA, SISTER MARY:
Fatima in Lucia's Own Words, Augustine Publishing Co., Chulmleigh (Devon), 1976.

MAILS, THOMAS E:
Fools Crow, Avon Books, New York, 1980.

MARCHI, JOHN DE:
Fatima from the Beginning, Augustine Publishing Co., Chulmleigh (Devon), 1981.

MILAREPA:
The Message of Milarepa, New Light upon the Tibetan Way (A Selection of poems translated from the Tibetan by Sir Humphrey Clarke), John Murray, 1958.

MURATA, SACHIKO:
The Tao of Islam, A Sourcebook on Gender Relationships in Islamic Thought, State University of New York Press, 1992.

NASR, SEYYED HOSSEIN:
Three Muslim Sages, Caravan Books, 1986.
An Introduction to Islamic Cosmological Doctrines, State University of New York Press, 1993.
Ideals and Realities of Islam, ABC International Group, 2000.
Man and Nature (The Spiritual Crisis of Modern

Man), ABC International Group, 1997.
Science and Civilization in Islam, Islamic Texts Society, 1987.
Islam and the Plight of Modern Man, ABC International Group, 2000.
Islamic Science: An Illustrated Study, World of Islam Festival Trust, 1976.
Western Science and Asian Cultures, Indian Council for Cultural Relations, New Delhi, 1976.
Sufi Essays, ABC International Group, 1999.
Knowledge and the Sacred (The Gifford Lectures, 1981), State University of New York Press, 1989.
Islamic Art and Spirituality, Golgonooza Press, 1987.
Islamic Life and Thought, State University of New York Press, 1981.
Traditional Islam in the Modern World, Kegan Paul International, 1987.
The Need for a Sacred Science, State University of New York Press, 1993.
Religion and the Order of Nature, Oxford University Press, 1996.
The Spiritual and Religious Dimension of the Environmental Crisis, Temenos Academy Papers, no. 12, 1999.

NEIHARDT, JOHN G:
Eagle Voice, Andrew Melrose, 1953.
Black Elk Speaks, University of Nebraska Press, 1988.

NORTHBOURNE, LORD:
Religion in the Modern World, Sophia Perennis, 1999.
Looking back on Progress, Sophia Perennis, 1995.

PALLIS, MARCO:

The Way and the Mountain, (second edition augmented), Peter Owen, 1994.
Peaks and Lamas, Woburn Press, 1974.
A Buddhist Spectrum, Allen and Unwin, 1980.

PERRY, WHITALL N:

A Treasury of Traditional Wisdom, Quinta Essentia, 1991, Fons Vitae, 2000.
The Widening Breach, Evolution in the Mirror of Cosmology, Quinta Essentia, 1995.
Challenges to a Secular Society, The Foundation for Traditional Studies, 1996.

PITMAN, MICHAEL:

Adam and Evolution, Rider, 1984.

RAMANA MAHARSHI:

Talks with Sri Ramana Maharshi (3 vols., O. Sri Ramasraman), Tiruvannamalai, 1955.

RŪMĪ, JALĀL AD-DĪN:

The Mathnawī of Jalālu'ddīn Rūmi (ed. and trans. R. A. Nicholson in 6 vols., the trans. being in vols. 2, 4 and 6), Gibb Memorial Trust, 1982.
Discourses of Rumi (translated and annotated by A. J. Arberry), Curzon, 1993.

SALES, LORENZO:

Jesus Appeals to the World, St. Paul Publications, 1958.

SANCHEZ-VENTURA Y PASCUAL, F:

The Apparitions of Garabandal, San Miguel Publications, Detroit, 1965.

SCHAYA, LEO:

The Universal Meaning of the Kabbala, Allen and Unwin, 1971.

SCHUMACHER, E F:

Small is Beautiful, Vintage, 1991.
A Guide for the Perplexed, Sphere Books, 1978.

SCHUON, FRITHJOF:

The Transcendent Unity of Religions (revised edition), Theosophical Publishing House, 1993.
Spiritual Perspectives and Human Facts (new translation), Sophia Perennis, 1987.
Gnosis: Divine Wisdom, Sophia Perennis, 1990.
Language of the Self, World Wisdom Books, 1999.
Stations of Wisdom, World Wisdom Books, 1995.
Understanding Islam, World Wisdom Books, 1998.
Light on the Ancient Worlds, World Wisdom Books, 1994.
Treasures of Buddhism, World Wisdom Books, 1993.
Dimensions of Islam, World Wisdom Books, 2000.
Islam and the Perennial Philosophy, World of Islam Festival Trust, 1976.
Esoterism as Principle and as Way, Sophia Perennis, 1990.
Castes and Races, Sophia Perennis, 1981.
Sufism: Veil and Quintessence, World Wisdom Books, 1981.
From the Divine to the Human, World Wisdom Books, 1982.
Logic and Transcendence, Sophia Perennis, 1985.
Christianity/Islam, World Wisdom Books, 1985.
The Essential Writings of Frithjof Schuon, Element, 1991.

Survey of Metaphysics and Esoterism, World Wisdom Books, 1986.
In the Face of the Absolute, World Wisdom Books, 1994.
The Feathered Sun: Plains Indians in Art and Philosophy, World Wisdom Books, 1990.
To Have a Center, World Wisdom Books, 1990.
Roots of the Human Condition, World Wisdom Books, 1991.
Images of Primordial and Mystic Beauty: Paintings by Frithjof Schuon, Abodes, 1992.
Echoes of Perennial Wisdom, World Wisdom Books, 1992.
The Play of Masks, World Wisdom Books, 1992.
The Transfiguration of Man, World Wisdom Books, 1995.
Road to the Heart, Poems, World Wisdom Books, 1995

SHASTRI, HARI PRASAD:
Echoes of Japan, 1916-1919, Shanti Sadan, London, 1983.
The World within the Mind, Shanti Sadan, London,1946.
The Heart of Eastern Mystical Teachings (originally published under the title *Sri Dada*), Shanti Sadan, London, 1950.

SHUTE, EVAN:
Flaws in the Theory of Evolution, Craig Press, Nutley, N J, 1961.

SINGAM, S DURAI RAJA:
The Wisdom of Ananda Coomaraswamy, Petaling Jaya, Malaysia, 1985.

SMITH, HUSTON:

Forgotten Truth: The Primordial Tradition, Harper & Row, 1976.

The World's Religions, Harper San Francisco, 1992.

Why Religion Matters, Harper San Francisco, 2001.

SMITH, WOLFGANG:

Cosmos and Transcendence, Sherwood Sugden, 1984.

Teilhardism and the New Religion, Tam Books, 1988.

The Quantum Enigma: Finding the Hidden Key, Sherwood Sugden, 1996.

STAVELEY, LILIAN:

The Golden Fountain, World Wisdom Books, 1982.

The Prodigal Returns, Watkins, 1921.

STODDART, WILLIAM:

Sufism: The Mystical Doctrines and Methods of Islam, Paragon, 1984.

Outline of Hinduism, Foundation for Traditional Studies, 1993.

Outline of Buddhism, Foundation for Traditional Studies, 1998.

Index